The Social Origins of English Education

THE STUDENTS' LIBRARY OF EDUCATION

The Social Origins of English Education

by Joan Simon

LONDON
ROUTLEDGE & KEGAN PAUL

First published 1970
by Routledge & Kegan Paul Ltd
Broadway House,
68-74 Carter Lane,
London EC4V 5EL
Printed in Great Britain by
Northumberland Press Ltd
Gateshead

ISBN 0 7100 6945 6 (c)
ISBN 0 7100 6946 4 (p)

THE STUDENTS' LIBRARY OF EDUCATION has been designed to meet the needs of Students of Education at Colleges of Education and at University Institutes and Departments. It will also be valuable for practising teachers and educationists. The series takes full account of the latest developments in teacher-training and of new methods and approaches in education. Separate volumes will provide authoritative and up-to-date accounts of the topics within the major fields of sociology, philosophy and history of education, educational psychology, and method. Care has been taken that specialist topics are treated lucidly and usefully for the non-specialist reader. Altogether, the Students' Library of Education will provide a comprehensive introduction and guide to anyone concerned with the study of education, and with educational theory and practice.

J. W. TIBBLE

By going back to the origins of English education in tribal society this book breaks new ground. There results a wider understanding of the ways in which the younger generation has been, and is, educated than can be conveyed by describing schools which only a minority ever entered, or which, even today, provide only a part of education. The author has already approached the question of what education is, and the function it performs in society, from various angles—by translating from the Russian work by psychologists on speech and child mental development which has had much influence (1959, 1963), in *Education and Society in Tudor England* (1966) accepted by historians as a standard work, and by research into the local history of education published in *Education in Leicestershire* (1968). In the present book she once more treats the history of education as an aspect of social and intellectual history, rather than the record of a closed educational world. The first part surveys educational developments up to the twelfth century, the second concentrates on particular aspects—rural upbringing, the new concept of education that arose in the town, the teaching methods of the medieval university, some of which are still with us. In each case use is made of specialist studies of a kind rarely drawn upon though they throw much light on changing educational concepts and forms of education.

BRIAN SIMON

Contents

Preface

There are many different definitions of education, arrived at from as many points of view. One method of approach is to look at education on the ground, through history, and try to assess it in these terms. The upbringing, or education, of the young is necessary in all human societies, and, with the help of anthropology, it is possible to begin with primitive origins and go on from there.

To consider the nature and function of education at different stages of social development is particularly relevant at a time when traditional systems are being transformed in many developing countries. By comparison, forms of education developed very slowly in England, and, for this very reason, there is still much that is traditional about our educational institutions and thinking. Historical study can throw light on this as well as on educational change.

The past only becomes interesting when there is an historical approach. Textbook accounts of early developments in education are often dull because they see the distant past in terms of the present. Instead of asking what education meant to early English society, and the forms that became established as a result, they look for the original secondary, or elementary, school long before anyone thought in these terms. This is to start off on the wrong foot. Since for centuries only a small proportion of children ever saw the inside of a classroom, there were forms of education much more influential than schools. To leave all these out of account is to obscure the base from which the modern system of education developed.

New developments in historical scholarship offer an opportunity to recast the history of education as an aspect of social and intellectual history, instead of concentrating on a supposedly closed educational world. This can only be a long process, but meanwhile it is possible to suggest a new starting point which opens up the whole field of education for consideration. This is the intention of this short book.

The first part surveys the early development of education in England, in broad outline, up to the twelfth century. In the second part three main topics are taken up in more detail, drawing on recent historical monographs which bear closely on education from different points of view. This is one way of taking account of new materials as a move towards keeping the history of education up to date. Other relevant studies are listed in the notes and bibliography.

I am much indebted for comments and criticisms to Peter Worsley, Professor of Sociology at Manchester University, and to the editor of the history section of the Students' Library of Education to which this is a contribution. The format of the series excludes an index, but there is a detailed contents list.

J. S.

Part One

1
The early development of education in England

As it has so far been written, the history of English education does not have a proper starting point. Either accounts begin with the organized schools of Greece and Rome, or with the arrival in England in 597 of a small band of Christian missionaries whose influence did not extend far beyond Kent. What really needs consideration, if we are interested in the origins of English education, is the nature or customs of Anglo-Saxon society and what these implied in terms of bringing up the new generation. Then it is possible to follow through the ways in which traditional custom was modified or new forms of education introduced.

Approach to the subject

To take society as a starting point in this way is to set aside the idea, borrowed from biology, which underlies much theorizing in the educational world. This is that human development depends on the interaction of heredity and environment, in just the same way as does the development of animals. Indeed, it is now fashionable to rewrite history in terms of biology or genetics, as if society were little more than a human zoo. The historian cannot accept this kind of reduction to the animal level which runs contrary to all that the historical record illustrates, least of all the historian of education.

Human beings do not merely adapt to a natural environment but create a social environment which stands between them and nature. In so doing, they follow a mode of life quite different from that of animals, and the experience of the species is acquired, accumulated and transmitted in an altogether different way. It is accumulated in the form of language and in all kinds of inanimate objects which incorporate human thought and action—tools, houses, clothes, as well as, eventually, books, radio-telescopes and the rest. This experience is transmitted by education, a key function of every human society from the most primitive stage.

In the animal world the experience of the species is transmitted by the infinitely slow process of heredity. The general picture is of slow biological evolution, in the form of adaptation of the species to the given environment, extending over millions of years. By contrast, the historical evolution of human society produces many changes within centuries.

This is because the experience of the human species is accumulated and transmitted not in a biological but in a social form, so altering the environment and bringing new influences to bear. In the process of acquiring this form of experience human beings acquired the corresponding mechanisms of behaviour in biological terms, differing from those of animals. In particular, physiologists describe the human brain as infinitely plastic. Its working is not merely modified from the animal state but transformed to correspond with the leading importance

4

in human behaviour of speech.[1]

The human child acquires the experience of mankind by the same kind of process as that by which this experience has been accumulated. He does not merely adapt to his social environment—as animals adapt to the natural environment—but actively engages with it, mastering practical activities and language. This is the process of human learning, promoted by education which is essential to the continuance of society from the earliest times.

In literate and advanced societies the transmission of experience is highly organized in educational institutions, as accumulated knowledge is also ordered and categorized. But there still continue basic forms of upbringing, or education, in family household and locality which have played a powerful part since the beginnings of human society.

Terminology has lagged behind growing knowledge of these different aspects. The word 'learning' is indiscriminately used for many different processes at quite different levels—from adaptation to new environmental conditions by rats in cages to the activities of universities of international standing. This facilitates the descent back into biology and it is still, strangely, imagined in some quarters that the best way to understand how children learn is to study the behaviour under stimulus of captive rats or pigeons. Were this so, there would be no call to write the history of education.

Some light is thrown on that history by the fact that in some languages the same word does duty for 'learning' and 'teaching', two sides of the same medal. On the other hand there are sometimes two words distinguishing 'education by upbringing' and 'education by instruction'. In practice, there is little distinction between these

5

two insofar as adults invariably teach the small child the elements of behaviour in a humanized world; for instance, to hold a spoon for certain purposes or to pronounce words in particular circumstances. But there is an important distinction at a later age in terms of forming active and mental behaviour, especially when knowledge becomes more extensive and is imparted in an organized way, by skilled teaching, in schools.

As an economic historian has recently noted, in studying the development of literacy in western Europe, 'the more a society develops, the greater is the role played by formal schools and formal teachers'.[2] During the period with which we are concerned organized education, in this sense, played a small part. But this does not mean that there is nothing to be found out about the education of children even though there are few or no documents describing it directly. When materials are lacking to follow a linear development it is possible to turn to the comparative method, and it is here that anthropology comes in.

Initiation in tribal society: the point of departure

All societies, however primitive, have recognized forms of bringing up children corresponding to their way of life. Anthropologists have shown this in detail, laying particular emphasis on initiation rites whereby the young are admitted to adult status at the base of a social system graded by seniority. These rites usually crown a period of particular preparation and the form they take illustrates the function education is intended to fulfil. They, therefore, throw a good deal of light, in turn, on the nature of the society.

Anthropologists, however, have chiefly studied isolated primitive societies with little stimulus to development, in which initiation tends to be ritualistic, or the conservative aspect of education is predominant. What we need to know about the progressive differentiation of education, in a developing society, cannot be learned from Margaret Mead.

On the other hand, a main line of development has been traced, from tribal custom to the organized educational systems of the Greek city states, and this has served as a guide to interpreting developments in northern Europe in a later age. Students of Greek literature, religion and society, drawing on anthropological findings, have suggested the following progression.[3]

In primitive tribal society, initiation is one of the most important social rites, a rite closely linked with that of marriage. Its function is to pass on the social experience of the community as a preliminary to admitting youth to adult status, a function expressed in primitive thought in the belief that the child dies as a child to be reborn as a man. This belief is concretely reflected in the form of initiation ceremonies which can be very complex— involving trials or ordeals and ritual disfigurement—and these are usually immediately followed by marriage.

At a higher stage of tribal society the practice of initiation is much modified, leaving a recognized form of training for all young men before marriage under the supervision of the elders. This is likely to comprise instruction in warlike dances or sports and in behaviour in adult company, particularly at ceremonies connected with communal meals, or feasting and hospitality. From such practices a direct continuity can be traced to the organized educational forms of Dorian Crete, Sparta and Athens.

7

These three systems of education may be seen as successive stages in the development of more sophisticated ways of preparing youth for life in a city state.

It was Cretan practice to bring boys of seventeen together into a group or 'herd' and train them in hunting, running, mock fights and the national war dance. Each youth was assigned a young man as guardian and with him entered the 'men's house' of the tribal settlement and joined in the young men's activities. His coming of age was finally marked by marriage, evidently a public ceremony covering a whole age group.

Under the more developed system of Sparta there were more distinct stages and marriage had ceased to mark its end in the same way. Boys remained under parental care until the age of seven. They were then enrolled in an *agéla* (herd) of their own age group and for some years followed a special course of life under the direction of the elders; their status was marked by shaving of the head. At twelve they were assigned to a young man as guardian with whom they entered into a lifelong relationship. At seventeen, they were promoted to an older group, with a recognized leader in early manhood who supervised games and fights. He also presided at the communal meals and after them taught the community's songs and gave instruction about public affairs. A year of this training was followed, at 18, by two years of more rigorous preparation including the ordeal of public scourging. At twenty the young man was admitted to the 'men's house' for common meals; only after this did marriage take place, but not as a universal ceremony.

Information about the Athenian system of education dates mainly from the end of the fourth century B.C. when earlier practices had been greatly modified. Young boys were trained in gymnastics under a *gymnasíarchos,* whose origin can be traced back to the tribal past. Promotion to an older group took place at eighteen, a year later than in Sparta and the two years' training that followed covered a public duty in the form of military service on the frontiers. This ended with a test marking the transition to full civic status. Eventually when military duties were abolished in Athens, after loss of its autonomy, organized academic education began to supplement athletics and social training.

Historians are often at a loss to explain the achievements of the educational system that resulted, and tend to fall back on the 'genius' of the peoples who then inhabited Greece, mixed though they were in racial origin. More relevant is the fact that the speed of the transition from a tribal organization to the civilized city-state provided a unique stimulus to, and opportunities for, understanding the nature of the world. In this connection it has been noted that the word 'cosmos', used by Greek philosophers to denote a sophisticated understanding of 'the order of nature', derived from the same root as the word which, in the earlier Greek of Homer, denoted the marshalling of clans for war and the settlement of tribes on the land.[4]

For a complex of reasons the Greek city state was the first literate society, in the sense that forms of government depended on the literacy of a substantial proportion of the male urban population. In place of the former oral tradition there was a wide use of writing, with all that it implies in terms of more exact knowledge and an objective approach to knowledge—out there on the page.[5] This was the foundation for great achievements in scholarship which began with the recording and criticism of the legacy of the tribal past. In the process, categories of learning were established which are only now being superseded, with the present explosion of knowledge.

The crown of the system of education established was the university of Athens which drew students from many parts of the Roman empire. Its legacy, preserved after the fall of Rome by the Christian church in east and west, was to be the key stimulus to intellectual development in the Europe of a later age.

Within the Roman empire, and around its borders, were many tribal societies in no position to move from tribalism to developed forms of urban civilization, but whose way of life was much modified by contact and conflict with a highly civilized imperial centre. Among these were the Germanic peoples who took part in the great migrations of the fifth century and turned the island of Britain into England. Students of Anglo-Saxon language and literature, ethnographers, archaeologists, historians, have contributed to discovering what was the direction of social development, or how the institutions of tribal society disintegrated, in this case. The picture they have drawn must be our starting point, for the Anglo-Saxon settlers drove the British inhabitants to outlying areas, or enslaved them, so that their social forms were dominant in the new setting.

Of the learning of Greece and Rome, these people knew nothing, but they had a well-established culture of their own and a pantheon of tribal gods. In the seventh century Christian missionaries brought knowledge of a universal religion and a heritage of learning which was rapidly assimilated at a time when permanent settlement on the land was posing new problems. But this could only modify, not determine, social development.

What took place was an active interpenetration of Germanic-tribal custom and Roman-Christian tradition from which there emerged the distinctive culture of the medieval period.

By the later middle ages this had developed as a culture so original, so far removed from any mere continuation of the laws and learning of the ancient world, that sixteenth-century reformers could claim that the wisdom of antiquity had been buried and find in classical literature the antithesis of the scholasticism they despised.[6] Equally, so skilfully had Christian practice been grafted on to, or merged with, the age-old observances of the people, that Protestant reformers, in their efforts to extinguish Roman Catholic practices, courted unpopularity by criticizing almost every popular amusement.

The key to understanding many later contradictions lies, therefore, in making a proper beginning.

The customs of Germanic society

In the first century the Roman historian Tacitus recorded observations about the social institutions of Germanic tribes. He described a barbarian social code which was still operating, in its essentials, in seventh century England when written records begin. Among other things, he witnessed a form of initiation for young warriors.

No youth could take up arms, wrote Tacitus, 'until the state has attested that he is likely to make good'. This implies the usual form of preliminary training, including trials or ordeals, before youths qualified for admittance to adult status in the tribe. Tacitus goes on to explain that boys who had proved themselves fit to become warriors were admitted at a special ceremony, after which they took up the life of companion to a warrior leader.[7]

> One of the chiefs, or the father or a kinsman equips the young man with shield and spear in the public council. This with the Germans is the equivalent of our *toga*—the first public distinction of youth. They cease to rank merely as members of the household and are now members of the state.... They are attached to the other chiefs, who are more mature and approved, and no one blushes to be seen thus in the ranks of the companions.

Commenting on this, the writer adds:

> There is intense rivalry among the companions for the first place by the chief, among the chiefs for the most numerous and enthusiastic companions. Dignity and power alike consist in being continually attended by a corps of chosen youths. This gives you consideration in peace-time and security in war.

The description tallies with other forms of evidence. In the declining age of the Roman empire a warlike form of organization became permanent among Germanic tribal peoples, superimposed on earlier social forms associated with the practice of agriculture. In time warrior rulers became permanently established and this undermined a former way of life, bonded by kinship, ruled by tribal elders and reflected in ancestor worship or the veneration of agricultural deities.

Tribal communities on the periphery of the empire were drawn into conflict at various levels, with each other and with imperial armies from which rich spoils could be gained. In the process tribal 'kings' emerged as supreme chiefs who claimed allegiance from their leading warriors in return for gifts and treasure gained by war. The bond of allegiance, of personal adherence to a leader, became the most potent tie among what became a warrior class, and warriors transformed the ancestral cult into worship of gods in their own image, among whom the god of battle held a prominent place. This particular stage of social development, or tribal disintegration, which gives rise to corresponding forms of religion and literature, has been designated the Heroic Age.[8]

A similar stage of development in the eastern Mediterranean man centuries before, when a tribal people plundered a rich civilization, is described in the Homeric poems glorifying the exploits of the Achaean warriors and their gods. These are more familiar, given the heavy classical bias of education over centuries, than the names of gods and warriors of the northern peoples and their literature, of which the outstanding example is the heroic poem *Beowulf*.

The focal point of such epics is the exploits of warrior heroes and their bands of 'companions'. They have little to say of the way of life among the main body of tribal followers who continued to work on the land and among whom kinship remained the overriding social bond. But with the settlement in England this older social practice comes to light. Now warriors were gradually transformed into landowners, their followers into cultivators of the land living in village communities, and it is in this setting that forms of upbringing can be traced.

There is no mention in the records of Anglo-Saxon, or Frankish, society of any ceremony of initiation for young warriors corresponding to that described by Tacitus. This should not be taken to imply that the custom ceased to prevail in the intervening centuries, and indeed there are traces pointing back to it.

It was the right to bear arms that distinguished free-man from serf in feudal society and it may well be that the ceremonial investiture of the liberated serf with spear and lance, the arms of the freeman, was the rem-nant of a once general practice. This enfranchisement has been described as a solemn and public act, performed in church or market place, the former serf being shown the ways and open gates as the arms were placed in his hands.[9]

It is usual for a dominant social practice, once out-moded, to become the province of the lower ranks of society. On the other hand, it has been suggested that even the sophisticated chivalric ceremonial associated with knighthood from the eleventh century should be traced back to an ultimate origin in the tribal practice of initiation to a warrior band.[10]

It is worth recalling also what Tacitus, the cultivated Roman admiring barbarian simplicities, as romantics were later to do, had to say about the children in Ger-manic tribal settlements in the first century:

They grow up in every home, naked and dirty, to that strength of limb and size of body which excite our admiration. Every mother feeds her child at the breast and does not depute the task to maids and nurses. The master is not to be distinguished from the slave by any pampering in his upbringing. They grow up together.

Describing the prevailing form of kinship, he under-lines how this led to the valuing of children:

A man's heirs and successors are his own children, and there is no such thing as a will; where there are no children, the next to succeed are, first, brothers, and then uncles, first on the father's, then on the mother's side. The larger a man's kin and the greater the number of his relations by marriage, the stronger is his influence when he is old. Childlessness ... is not a paying profession.

While forms of kinship varied, this wide range of inter-relationship is typical of the tribal stage of social organization.

The settlement in England: two forms of upbringing

It was a tribal host representing the form of society described earlier that settled in England, a society in which there was evidently a clear division between warrior chiefs, who appear to have constituted an hereditary nobility, and the main body of followers. When sections of the invading host took possession of different areas, demarcating them as kingdoms, kings rewarded their leading adherents with land instead of treasure. Under the conditions of settlement on the land the personal bond between lord and adherent was gradually replaced by new quasi-feudal relations, depending on tenure of land. These extended to cover the tribal followers who settled in villages to till the soil and engage in agricultural crafts.

From Anglo-Saxon laws it is clear that the bond of kinship still governed the way of life and outlook at all levels of society in the seventh and eighth centuries. The precise nature of the kindred is still a matter for discussion.[11] But there was in English society, in historic times, no clan of the Celtic type, nor was the social unit exclusively patriarchic or agnatic like the Roman *gens*, i.e. with all rights centred on male descent. By the time laws were formulated, the basic unit may well have been the three or four-generation patriarchal family which usually succeeds the broader kindred group when economic life has advanced to a stage allowing for the accumulation of inheritable wealth. But, whatever the group designated by the term 'kindred' in Anglo-Saxon law, the kin still exercised a social function of great importance, extending to cover the upbringing of youth.

Again, we should begin with the lower ranks of society to find the oldest form. Among the communities of freemen, settled on the land and working in agriculture, kinship persisted as the chief social bond, to be modified in time by the new ties of neighbourhood in the village and service to a lord of the manor. This implies, in turn, that the upbringing of children devolved on the family household within the village community.

An early popular verse illustrates an attitude towards young children common in tribal societies, where the end of childhood is often marked by the appearance of the second teeth at about the age of seven: 'One shall not rebuke a youth in his childhood, until he can reveal himself. He shall thrive among the people in that he is confident.'[12] The earliest Anglo-Saxon laws indicate that the kindred bore responsibility for minors, even to the extent of protecting a child from his own father. If the father died, the child remained with his mother and the kindred administered his property until he attained adult status. This continued to be the practice among freemen throughout the medieval period.

When, with the growth of towns, popular practice comes to the surface in this new setting, communal provision for the orphans of citizens is to be found, and in due course of time for the education of all sons of freemen in the borough school. On the other hand, all that can be discerned of earlier practice in the countryside is the participation of youth in special festivals, such as that of Mayday, some aspects of which are clearly linked with mating and marriage.

There is more to go on in the sphere of the dominant warrior nobility, where allegiance had overlaid the ancient obligations of kinship. Here the progression was through upbringing in the family household, or that of a superior lord, initially under the women, then through active military service to settlement on the land.

In *Beowulf* the hero recounts that he was sent at the age of seven to the court of King Hrethel, his grandfather.[13]

> I was seven years old when the prince of treasures, the friendly ruler of the peoples, took me from my father; King Hrethel brought me up, bestowed on me treasure and banqueting, bore in mind our kinship; in his life I was no less loved by him, a child in the court, than any of his children.

Possibly the young child at court was assigned to a particular member of the household, as Achilles was placed under the guidance of Phoenix at a comparable stage of social development in Greece.[14] This itself was an adaptation of tribal practice in a particular setting. 'Do you remember,' Phoenix asks Achilles in his tent at the gates of Troy, 'how you would refuse to go out to dinner or to touch your food at home with anyone but me ... Yes, I went through a great deal for you and worked hard.' And he also reminds his former charge that he is still his guardian, appointed by the father when the Trojan expedition set out, for you were a mere lad, with no experience of the hazards of war, nor of debate, where people make their mark. It was to teach you all these things, to make a speaker of you and a man of action, that he sent me with you.

This brings out what were necessary accomplishments at the courts of Anglo-Saxon kings. Besides training in warlike pursuits, the art of speaking at councils of warriors was of much importance and there was also an elaborate etiquette to learn. The young thane was bound to defend his lord to the last in battle, at home to be his hearth companion and confidant, join him in hunting and other active pursuits and serve him personally at feasts during the evening.

The stress on personal companionship waned in later years but the other elements remained in the training of the nobility, including that of domestic service. Up to the fifteenth century and beyond, books inculcating 'manners' often revolve around personal valeting, or the arts of carving and serving at table, for communal feasting remained a characteristic feature at all levels of the social order.[15] The idea that even the heir to a great name and fortune has, as a youth, the status of servant became firmly established. It would seem to derive from the particular way in which the traditional preparation for adult life was modified within the aristocratic household.

In the Heroic Age, when the young companion attained manhood, at the comparatively late age of twenty-four or so, his lord was expected to provide an estate so that he might set up his own household. Once of age the young knight, as he now was, might seek service under a neighbouring king in the hope of marrying a daughter, and achieving a share in the sovereignty of which he personally disposed—a situation familiar enough from innumerable folk tales.

In course of time, with the establishment of feudal landownership and the evolution of property rights or laws of inheritance, the succession to land became fixed and disposal in marriage the rule. This is illustrated by the system of wardship which extended to cover all men who held land in return for military service, or by the tenure of 'knight service'.

The orphaned son of any man holding land by this feudal tenure became the ward, not of his kindred as in the case of freemen, but of the lord to whom he owed homage for his lands, until he came of age at twenty one. Meanwhile the lord took control of his property, supervised his upbringing, and could arrange his marriage; girls were under supervision until the marriageable age of fourteen.[16] These rights were often abused, but the implication is that the responsibilities undertaken were the recognized ones of fathers of families. Later, however it became a general practice to send both boys and girls away to a household of higher social standing for their upbringing, as a good way both of getting training and a start in life under influential patronage.

Settlement produced a modification of the concept of nobility by blood, developed in the Heroic Age, in favour of a concept related to the new reality—that nobility derives from ownership of land. Under the feudal order it was in return for land that allegiance (or fealty) was accorded, or homage paid. Since land was held on condition of giving military service when required, the old obligation remained at one remove. But a new social form was needed to weld together the warriors of a more complex society which had other leading interests and concerns.

This was provided by knighthood, as it developed in the eleventh and twelfth centuries, in close association with increased use of the horse and riding. Here was a mystical brotherhood-in-arms for which an elaborate form of initiation was created, to which the church added its blessing.[17]

Chivalric training has often been seen as the main form of noble upbringing, as if future landowners needed only instruction in military skills and behaviour of a ceremonial kind. But just as the young companion of an earlier age must learn to speak at councils, so the future lord of the manor must understand the elements of law and government however many his servants. There was always an intellectual content to the upbringing of the nobility, even if not necessarily imparted by way of formal teaching.

The great households of the middle ages were the centre of secular pursuits of all kinds, at many levels, with their literate clerks and stewards as well as knights and retainers. Insofar as they were a microcosm of the world, they imparted a knowledge of the world of affairs to a younger generation which would be concerned with government.

New influences: the conversion of the English kingdoms

It was at a moment when Anglo-Saxon society was adapting to a new form of development associated with permanent settlement on the land—though wars between the different kingdoms were still frequent—that the influence of the Christian religion and the learning that churches had preserved were brought to bear.

The first missionaries to make a general impression in the seventh century came from Ireland where Christianity had survived from an earlier age, in monastic communities which constituted a clan in tribal settlements. The traditions preserved and modified by Irish monks in this setting diverged from those at the centre in Rome with which there had long been no contact. In particular they had no idea of territorial bishoprics, or establishing a diocesan system. Irish missionaries went among the English people as among their own, particularly in the north-eastern kingdom of Northumbria, learned their language and preached an evangelistic message in simple terms. Familiar with an ascetic way of life they preferred to establish monastic communities rather than live at the courts of kings. Their skills in writing and illumination of manuscripts drew admiration from Anglo-Saxons who themselves had developed art forms and some acquaintance with writing. Their stories of the fathers of the church, the gospel story itself and observances connected with it, approximated to tribal lore in various ways and had a strong attraction.

Since war was no longer the only business of the upper ranks of society, the culture associated with it, the gods who presided over it, were that much less relevant to kingly courts and a universal god quite readily acceptable. But understanding came only gradually and the first kings converted went to war in the name of the new god, vowing to give gold to found monasteries, or to hand over daughters to a virgin life, in return for victory.

The Christian practice of infant and adult baptism corresponded to the two forms of initiation known to tribal society, initiation in youth, already discussed, and 'adoption' in manhood which was also accompanied by special rites. It also echoed old beliefs in proclaiming that, through baptism, men die to sin and are born to righteousness. This was a mystical rite, a preparation not so much for social life as the world to come; but to a tribal people baptism implied adoption into a wider community with rules of its own to be observed. These were the more easily acceptable in that, while requiring the modification of longstanding customs, they introduced new skills or knowledge of first importance to the government of a settled kingdom. By comparison with a predominantly oral record of custom, literacy and the associated organization of knowledge enabled the recording of laws, the beginnings of a conception of history, new forms of intellectual development in governing circles. The great work of scholarship of the Anglo-Saxon period is a history of the English nation and its conversion which applied scholarly rules in studying the recent tribal past.

This development was furthered by the Christian missions from Rome. Coming to a more or less unknown country, beyond the influence of the organized church in Gaul, they brought the new faith and the new knowledge direct to kingly courts. It is a primary aim of missionaries of an organized church—and the Roman church had a territorial form of organization centred on the bishop and his diocese—to convert tribal chiefs and secure recognition for this form of organization. Once the support of a king had been gained, and land granted to found the first churches, young nobles in attendance at court could be gathered together to be educated in the faith, to secure the church in the next generation.

It was in this way that Augustine's mission, a band of monks, established a foothold in Kent from 598, though it was only maintained with difficulty in later years.[18] But missionary activity spreading to some extent from here, from the Irish in the north, from Gaul, worked a gradual change, and improved communications helped to persuade English kings and their followers that adherence to Rome was in their interests. When a second mission arrived from there in 669, headed by two scholars, the way had been prepared for a centre of learning at Canterbury whose influence could spread. A young noble who studied here, Aldhelm, became one of the first native scholar-bishops, who, in turn, spread the learning they had gained. Another who studied at Canterbury, Benedict Biscop, founded a monastery in the north-east, Jarrow, which was to become the main centre of English scholarship in the eighth century.

Kings accepted the rank of bishop and accorded it a status equivalent to that of the thane, or lay noble. Early native bishops were often the kindred of ruling kings, educated to take a leading place in the new church, and their households could become centres for the education of another generation of young men of noble blood. Wilfrid, bishop of Ripon in the seventh century, was the first prince of the English church, living in state at home, travelling on missions to the Pope and taking a leading part in securing the agreement which consolidated the English church in allegiance to Rome. His household is said to have rivalled that of the king of Northumbria in magnificence and to have become 'a school where young nobles received their military education.'[19]

The same was to be said of the household of Thomas Becket, as archbishop of Canterbury in the twelfth century, and of Thomas Wolsey's following in the early sixteenth century. In short, bishops came to play a major

23

part in government and remained the right-hand men of kings down to the Reformation. Accordingly their households were second only to the royal court as a place of training for, and advance to, important positions in the kingdom. Equally, literate clerks became indispensable servants of kings, so embarking the church on the path of close integration with lay society and its administration at this level.

While the conversion profoundly modified methods of government, and kingly courts, it had a less immediate effect on the population. But the church, in establishing its sacraments of baptism, confirmation, marriage, burial —together with the mass as sustenance for the soul and penance to cleanse it—gradually took over regulation of the way of life. It was probably by laws relating to marriage and the family that it exercised the greatest influence on the lives of ordinary people.[20] In the thirteenth century enlightened bishops, scholars and statesmen though they now were, saw it as their task to spread good advice of the kind once handed down by elders of a close-knit tribal community. Parents must take care not to overlay babies, upset cradles, nor leave young children near fire or water.[21]

So far as the popular outlook was concerned, the abandoning of the religion of the Heroic Age in ruling circles appears to have produced a reversion to older forms, associated with life on the land, notably the veneration of female agricultural deities and magical rites.[22] That Christian teaching, of the kind conducted in the vernacular, had an effect is evident from the relics of simple instruction in folk song or tale. But doctrine had to be attuned to popular understanding; indeed the missionaries from Rome were expressly instructed not to ridicule old beliefs but to build upon them.[23] The outcome was that former ideas, which had governed the social outlook for many centuries, were supplemented by a new Christian magic rather than supplanted.

This may be seen in the popular festivals which continued to punctuate the agricultural year, centred on the invocation of spirits to ensure regeneration of the soil and a successful harvest. These retained traditional characteristics throughout the middle ages, with the addition of a Christian colour. But, as late as the fourteenth century, some popular songs associated with peasant uprisings bear strong traces of ritual origins and no mark of any Christian sentiment.[24] Others, though reflecting simple precepts, bear no trace of the sophisticated doctrine of the Roman church. Even in mid-sixteenth century seasonal rites were generally observed, to the despair of protestant reformers. Thus Philip Stubbes included Mayday ceremonies in his 'anatomy of abuses':[25]

> Against May . . . every parish, town and village assemble . . . they go some to the woods and groves . . . and . . . return bringing with them birch boughs . . . to deck their assemblies . . . but their chiefest jewel they bring from thence is their May-pole . . . and then they fall to banquet and feast, to leap and dance about it, as the heathen people did at the dedication of their idols, whereof this is a perfect pattern or rather the thing itself.

With the wide divergence between the way of life of lord and peasant went a progressively widening intellectual gulf, as literacy was present at one pole and absent at the other. Among the aristocracy traditional methods of upbringing, grounded on allegiance, were modified and enriched. For the peasantry the strong, slow-moving current of popular life, fed by oral tradition, was the background. Against this background the family household—with its numerous domestic and agricultural tasks —provided a certain pattern of upbringing.

Once again we may look forward to later practice in the towns where there developed a system of apprenticeship in service in the urban household under guild supervision. The guilds, formed under the patronage of a saint who took the place of a common ancestor, substituted for kinship by blood the bond of a common profession and assumed responsibilities for the education of the young. But apprenticeship evidently operated in detail long before the establishment of the regulated systems of the later middle ages. This suggests, in turn, a prevailing pattern of inducting youth to tasks within the household in the villages from which towns were recruited—a pattern still to be observed in the relatively primitive agricultural community where even small children have a given place by virtue of their economic contribution.

Monasteries: recruitment and scholarship

Much has been written about the monasteries which were the mainstay of the church in England for centuries, given the difficulty of establishing a diocesan organization. The monastic way of life, in brotherhood, had a strong appeal and drew many recruits. Its foundation, as laid down by the fathers of the church, was that 'no man said that he had anything of his own but they had all things in common'.[26]

However, it was not only those bound by monastic vows who lived communally. In the prevailing conditions this was essential for the clergy as a whole, whether in bishops' households or in the minsters set up to evangelize outlying areas. The word 'minster' is merely the Old English form of 'monastery', so there are no grounds here for drawing a sharp line between monks and clergy, as has sometimes been done. At this stage the main difference was that there was no prohibition on marriage for the minor clergy; this meant that communities of clergy were likely to break up into separate households, or were much less stable than those bound by monastic vows. On the other hand, many early monastic communities were small and casually organized, lacking any recognized form of discipline.

Communities of monks were under the paternal rule of an abbot, or abbess, at this time. Their members supported life by necessary agricultural work and assisted the needy, as well as maintaining services in church; and, where opportunity offered, they studied or copied manuscripts according to their ability. It was not necessary to be literate, let alone learned, to take to this way of life as a 'serf of God'; it was enough to learn to take part in a service by repetition and memorizing. But the well-organized monastery provided the necessary conditions for sustained scholarship by some, as Jarrow did for Bede. Learned monks were chosen for ordination as priests and undertook the preparation of others for the priesthood.

The two methods of recruitment to the monastic life, like baptism, derived from the two known methods of initiation. Either a child was 'offered' by his kinsmen as an oblate with an offering in kind—as was the first of English historians, Bede, at the age of seven. Or it was possible to be adopted in later life and serve a novitiate. The form of oblation, as laid down in the early eleventh century by the constitutions of archbishop Lanfranc, was as follows—the 'tonsure' being the ritual practice of cutting the hair in a special way.[27]

> If a child is to be offered to the monastery he shall be tonsured, and then, bearing in his hands a host and chalice with wine in it, as is the custom, he shall be offered by his parents after the Gospel to the priest celebrating Mass. When his offering has been received by the priest, his parents shall wrap the child's hands in the cloth which covers the altar and which hangs down in the front, and then the abbot shall accept him. When this is done the parents shall straightway promise . . . that the child shall never abandon the monastic life through their agency or that of anyone representing them. . . . This promise shall have been previously written down and witnessed, and now they shall make it verbally and then place it on the altar. When this is done the abbot shall bless a cowl and, taking off the child's cloak . . . shall say 'May the Lord strip thee of the ... old man' ... and, clothing him with the cowl, shall continue, 'May the Lord clothe thee with the new man'.

This rebirth was usually marked by taking a new name. The two ways of entry to the monastic order continued for many years, until child oblation was criticized and fell into disuse in the twelfth century, after which entrants were recruited in their teens. For the boy given by his kindred to the service of God, the bonds of kinship were severed. The close bond of the religious community replaced them, while more widely the church extended its protection over all the clergy, and, eventually, its law over all the literate.

Bede's outline of his life history is well known. Born

in the territory of the monastery of Jarrow, placed at the age of seven under the care of its abbot, Benedict, for his education, he daily observed the discipline including participation in the church services, studied scripture and 'always took delight in learning, teaching, and writing'.[28]

A rich library of manuscripts had been collected at Jarrow, allowing for study not only of the scriptures and fathers of the church but also of those classics of the ancient world which the church in the west had managed to preserve. An important task at this stage was to find a way of determining the date of Easter, a major matter of controversy between Irish and Roman churches, and other points of chronology. It was to such ends that study of arithmetic was cultivated.

Bede was evidently an inspired teacher, as well as devoted scholar, and his *Ecclesiastical History of the English Nation* had an educational intention.

'If history relates good things of good men,' he wrote in the preface—to a work which interspersed carefully researched narrative with stories of the Irish saints—'the attentive hearer is excited to imitate that which is good.' Throughout the middle ages all literature had a didactic purpose, a point which will be returned to later.

The regime of master teaching pupils became established in the well-organized monastery, and the custom of the master handing on his office to his favourite, or best, pupil. But it is unnecessary to think only in terms of birch-rods, later the schoolmaster's insignia. In early days boys came directly under the care of abbots. A poem addressed early in the ninth century to the abbot of a celebrated French monastery, by one of his former pupils, gives a pleasant picture.[29] The abbot is recalled, seated in a small garden close, in the green darkness of apple trees.

> And they would gather you the shining fruit
> With the soft down upon it; all your boys,
> Your little laughing boys, your happy school,
> And bring huge apples clasped in their two hands.

Again, a famous teacher at York, Alcuin, who left there in 782 to direct an educational revival from the court of Charlemagne, sent back an adjuration to the young novices of Jarrow which suggests everyday diversions. They must not, he said, 'be digging at foxes or chasing hares' but learn the sacred scriptures and 'take to heart the example of the youthful diligence of Bede'.[30]

At first there had been little opportunity for sustained scholarship, though there were some outstanding individual scholars, such as Aldhelm. But in the northern kingdom of Northumbria in the eighth century a body of learning was built up, and methods of teaching evolved, of which Charlemagne was glad to make use. The background was the lively vernacular culture in the north, while scholars could draw on both the Irish tradition of learning and the solid knowledge gained from the Roman church. This helps to account for the two schools of this period, representing a peak of achievement, the second a direct descendant of the first. These were in the monastery of Jarrow, where Bede taught, and at York, a school launched by his pupil, Egbert, a brother of the king of Northumbria, who became a bishop. A later master here was Alcuin.

It was the great achievement of teachers of this period in England that they provided Latin grammars adapted to the needs of pupils whose native tongue was Germanic.[31] Nor was rhetoric foreign to a vernacular culture whose main expression was poetic. Indeed, when Alcuin wrote dialogues for younger pupils he used the form of the native riddle.[32]

What is the body?	The spirit's lodging.
What is hair?	The clothing of the head.
What is the beard?	The distinction of the sexes, the mark of age.
What are the eyes?	The guides of the body, the vessels of light, the index to thought.
What is the sun?	The splendour of the world, the beauty of the sky, the grace of nature, the honour of the day, the distributor of the hours.
What is the sea?	The path of boldness, the earth's bourne, the divider of regions, the receiver of streams, the spring of showers.

To read these is not to think immediately either of classical culture or the Christian religion.

It was at a time when Northumbria reached a leading position among the English kingdoms, and the long-planned archbishopric of York was established, that the schools there achieved a reputation which carried to European courts. Bishop Egbert may have started the school at York for the clerks of his church, or household, but his teaching, in the tradition of his own master, attracted others and made York a centre of scholarship. Here, too, there was a library which included, with patriarchal and classical works, the modern writings of native English scholars such as Aldhelm and Bede. But by the close of the eighth century Northumbria had given way before the midland kingdom of Mercia, and in the ninth century Danish invasion overwhelmed the north and its foundations.

There was as little continuity of scholarship elsewhere in England at this time.[33] But the highest achievements had been transmitted to the Frankish court and there entered into a current of continental learning which survived the great upheavals of the Scandinavian invasions.

Bishops and initiation to the priesthood

Bishops, the fountainhead of the church's organization, were in early days directly responsible for all its activities. It was their duty to instruct the laity by sermons and administer the sacrament of baptism as well as confirmation, tasks eventually devolved on the parish clergy. But their chief responsibility was the instruction of new recruits to the priesthood. Ordination regenerated the body of the clergy; it was the spiritual counterpart of procreation.

The early church had perfected a system of initiation which involved passing through six grades, but by the seventh century three had been telescoped. Special preparation could begin at the age of seven when boys were tonsured. Then came the grades of acolyte, sub-deacon, deacon, at intervals of several years until orders were eventually taken at about the age of forty. Boys could be so prepared in the household of a bishop, or in monasteries which undertook organized teaching. But as the church expanded and became established on a territorial basis, with demarcated dioceses and parishes, the preparation of intending priests was also devolved, ordination took place earlier and it proved difficult to maintain standards.

To turn to the practical plane, and how churches were provided, is to appreciate the difficulties. To establish a church it was necessary for a king or thane to give land and gold and these were usually readily forthcoming. By the eleventh century, when Domesday Book provides information, there were many churches of various grades and the outline of a diocesan system.

But lay lords who financed building on their own land naturally tended to regard the resulting church as a personal possession and this militated against the organization of the church as an ecclesiastical body independent of lay influence. The church never managed to transcend the basic Germanic law that all that stood on the soil belonged to the owner of the soil; it could only come to terms with it.[34]

Just as kings made grants for cathedral churches, and accorded bishops a recognized place among their following, so lesser landowners provided a parish church, assumed the right of appointing a priest to serve it and treated him as a personal dependent. This meant that the parish priest had much closer links with an immediate lay lord than with a probably distant diocesan bishop, his superior in the church. Up to the thirteenth century many priests, in and of their local community, were married and handed down the office to their sons.[35]

In the circumstances the classic form of initiation to the priesthood must often have gone by default, at any rate so far as the stages of special instruction were concerned. Apart from the boys gathered under the eye of bishop or abbot, it devolved on parish priests to pick out promising boys of humble birth and begin preparing them for ordination. So long as schools were comparatively few, and the need for more clergy great, young men were

33

likely to be accepted for ordination to a parish church without any great claim to literacy or learning. In any case, in later centuries many parish priests were barely literate. Rather than instructing the laity by sermons, the primary duty devolved on them, they could only recite the offices of the church in a language never mastered.

On the other hand, a system of preparing boys of good birth for leading positions in the church was established in episcopal households, as well as greater monasteries, and it was at this level that an educated clergy was produced. As their diocesan duties increased bishops devolved the duty of teaching on to a master, or a school attached to the household or the cathedral church. When circumstances were favourable, and the master skilled, a centre of learning could develop, as at York and Canterbury.

Then, at a lower level, both cathedral churches and monasteries had to provide simple instruction in Latin and music for those conducting the daily services in church, and as a preparation for more advanced studies. This established the pattern of teaching that was to prevail in schools for boys throughout the middle ages, based on learning by heart the Latin psalter, or primer of prayers, and then going on to study the elements of Latin grammar.

Neither a centre of higher learning, nor a school to train young clerks in the liturgy, was an institution single-mindedly directed to preparing intending priests. These were forms of instruction adapted to training the lower clergy serving the churches of the great religious foundations and the higher clergy to administer these or carry on the church's work in the wider world. In short, in education as in other matters the church could not impose a given form of organization evolved in other circum-

34

stances and maintain it unchanged. As it took on much more than purely ecclesiastical duties in society, so the system of formal instruction established tended to lose the religious direction of preparation for holy orders in favour of teaching of a more general kind. Then the gap was bridged by calling any educated man a clerk, whether or not he was in orders.

Bishops did not remain in control of the chief schools established, for these were administered by religious foundations which became increasingly autonomous as they gained wealth and power, whether they were monastic or communities of clergy serving cathedral and other major churches. It was not from the cathedral church that bishops administered their dioceses but from their own households with the aid of attendant clerks, just as literate clerks in the households of kings and nobles supervised the machinery of secular government. It was to the wider needs of these occupations that higher education had to conform.

Hence, in the twelfth century, the universities—which superseded the centres of learning originally connected with monastery and cathedral, now criticized by the lively clerks of episcopal and noble households as behind the times. Cathedral schools in urban centres were the most open to change. Since the cathedral clergy now had many concerns they had in turn devolved the duty of keeping school on a master who hired a hall in the town in which to teach, and took little further interest in the matter. It was therefore possible for outside teachers to move in and conduct the new forms of teaching which turned relatively insignificant institutions into incipient universities.[36] Then there was a long struggle to break free from the authority which officers of the cathedral reimposed. This was the pattern in France, but the two universities in England became established in towns without any cathedral church.

Thus the system of formal education introduced under the auspices of the church was modified to serve the needs of society, rather than concentrating on a straightforward preparation for ecclesiastical duties. Nevertheless, the stages of education were roughly adjusted to the grades of advancement towards ordination, though this becomes clear only when the organization of both clergy and schools has reached a higher level—for instance, in the linking of the university degree of B.A. to deacon's orders and that of M.A. to the full orders of priest.

Invasion and reconstruction: conquest and feudal order

The Scandinavian invasions of the late ninth and tenth centuries shook all the kingdoms of Europe and laid waste many foundations in England, with all the eastern kingdoms. In the prevailing darkness of this period there is only a brief glimpse of the kingdom of Wessex, during a temporary lull before a renewed invasion of 892. This was ruled by Alfred, who pinned hopes for reconstruction on an educational programme extending beyond the rehabilitation of Latin scholarship to the promotion of literacy in the vernacular. Providing translations of some key works to assist the process, he expressed the wish that 'all the youth now in England of freemen, who are rich enough to be able to devote themselves to it, be set to learn ... until they are able to read English writing well'.

The inference is that there was a relatively large class of freemen in a position to put sons to school, and that the urgent needs of the time favoured efforts to merge learning, hitherto confined to scholars, with practical experience in the conduct of affairs. This was to draw on the best of two traditions: that of the tribal past when all freemen had access to the accumulated knowledge of the community, and that of the church which had imparted the learning necessary to good government to the few.[37]

When, in the tenth century, general reconstruction became possible, the emphasis was on monastic foundations, on a new model, which provided a basis for recreating arts and crafts as well as literacy and learning. The Benedictine monasteries founded at this time had an intimate connection at many points with the national life, including a rich vernacular culture, and turned outwards to the people in a way unknown on the continent.[38]

Monastic writers of this period developed vernacular prose and verse to a level not to be surpassed for another three centuries. Their schools for novices taught the arts of fine writing and illumination of manuscripts, as well as music and Latin. Moreover there survive from this time textbooks which, besides adapting the teaching of Latin grammar in the light of the vernacular, appreciate the need to relate learning to life.

The best known of these is the colloquy of Aelfric, written for the boys he taught in a Benedictine monastery, which takes as subject matter the daily work and way of life of ordinary people. Stress was laid on clear articulation by the Benedictine order and, after boys had learned the psalter by heart, they went on to practise pronunciation and learn the elements of grammar and syntax by way of colloquy with the master. He posed questions within the limits of their knowledge to draw a well-formulated reply. It may, therefore, be the kind of answers that the boys of Aelfric's school gave to his questions that provided the basis for his textbook—now an invaluable from the liberal arts.'[47]

Within a century the Norman Conquest had swept vernacular literature underground, and it was not to re-emerge, from beneath Norman-French and Latin, until the later middle ages. A compensation for the educated was that English clerks were now brought directly in touch with new theological and legal studies which had been developing on the continent for the past half-century. These began to be cultivated in monastic houses which now entered their last phase as the chief centres of learning. From these relatively isolated religious communities, whose scholarly interests were circumscribed accordingly, learning passed to an urban setting.

The Norman Conquest brought England under the rule of the most highly developed feudal principality in Europe. With the firming up of feudal law and forms of government, it becomes clear how closely the church was integrated with the social order in which it had gradually become established and with which it had developed. In effect, the church emerged as one of the estates of feudal society, and King Alfred's dictum that the kingdom comprised those who fought, those who worked and those who prayed became a commonplace of medieval thought.

The church had introduced formal methods of instruction for those who prayed, in Latin and in song, in the round of services maintained in monastery and cathedral. It had also provided the conditions for sustained scholarship as an adjunct of the religious life, while episcopal households provided a training related to administration of the church in the world. More generally, the church's influence spread over all forms of education, from the initiation of the young knight to the catechizing of the peasant child, for its rites had replaced those with which society had formerly sanctified social practice.

But there was no adequate system of induction for the parish clergy, just as it had proved impossible to secure them adequate remuneration and independence of lay patrons. While bishops ranked with lay lords, parish priests ranked on the whole with the peasantry from which most entrants necessarily came. They tilled the glebe for a livelihood which was only supplemented by the tithes of their own produce given by parishioners and the dues for burial and other services. Often they had little more education than the flock it was their duty to educate in the faith.

The poor, barely literate, parish priest could not provide the basic teaching necessary to prepare local boys in turn for ordination, as was his duty. If schools increased in number they were still relatively few and it was not easy for a village boy to get to one in a cathedral town or the almonry of a monastery unless circumstances were favourable. This hardly constituted an organized system of recruitment to the church; above all, its foundation was weak. The poverty and ignorance of the parish clergy were the Achilles' heel of the church, up to the Reformation and beyond. Meanwhile, more profitable positions in the church could fall to those with influence, or, even, those who paid for the privilege of an appointment.

The church underlined its monopoly of the means to learning by extending its protection over the literate, claiming all those who knew Latin as 'clerks' whether or not they were in orders. This was the definition of a clerk, one who was *literatus*, so that all students at universities eventually came within the category. Equally, benefactions to education, as to the church itself, came within the orbit of Christian charity.

The church had necessarily come to rule over the realm of scholarship. Only in settled communities of monks or clergy had there been occasion to tap the experience of the ancient world and make it available for current use, as well as studying the scriptures and the fathers of the church. When, however, the kingdoms of Europe emerged into a relatively settled period, with the end of the migrations and invasions which had marked the era of disintegrating tribalism, there were important technical advances, a new economic prosperity, and social organization took on more complex forms. So, too, did formal education which now came to contribute more directly to intellectual development in the community at large.

Town and country: the rise of universities

The foundation of medieval society was land and agriculture and this society is often described as static and unchanging. No doubt it was, for serfs tied to the soil, but even they saw something of an outside world which seems, at times, to have been constantly on the move. There was no need to go to London to see the king, when the royal court was in constant circulation and might be glimpsed on the nearest highway, for kings had to live off each of their manors in turn, nobles and bishops likewise. A bishop must also do the round of his diocese, pay visits to the capital in the course of his duties, sometimes travel as far as Rome. Many in all walks of life embarked on pilgrimages and there were no frontiers on the continent to bar the way. Nor was there any barrier for the educated who made a pilgrimage in search of new ideas and good teaching, rather than sacred relics, since all learning was in a common language.

Nearer home, men met at country fairs, local festivals, in the courtyard of castles, at the monastery gate, in the porch of cathedrals where legal cases were judged. On the roads were kings' messengers, knights and retainers, travelling merchants and artisans, friars who preached in the vernacular, minstrels and mimers, serfs delivering and collecting for the purposes of village and manor.

This intercommunication helps to explain a movement quite as significant as successive turns by scholars to study of the classical heritage, namely the repeated welling to the surface of popular tradition, until the 'vulgar tongue' became the language of the nation and its literature was born anew.

Earlier civilizations had centred on highly developed forms of urban life, in the midst of barbarism. In medieval Europe there was interplay between town and country. In England, in particular, towns merged into the countryside. Only the ports had a relatively large population, above all the capital which was itself a port, and approximated more nearly to the great merchant centres that developed on the continent with a standard of life well above that of the countryside.

Moreover, in the early middle ages the hall of castle or manor house was shared by the household, rather than reserved to its master and his family, and a gathering place for others as well. Hospitality was an ancient tradition, now a social and Christian duty, and manor houses as well as monastic houses provided food and shelter for wayfarers and alms for beggars.

In the circumstances much popular mythology passed into written literature in the twelfth century. Popular lyrics affected courtly styles and in the thirteenth-century dances such as the 'carole' passed from market place to castle hall. In music there was a constant inter-penetration of styles.

Nor were the activities of the greatest scholars altogether foreign to the ordinary man. In the popular estimation those who engaged in new mathematical or scientific studies, in the thirteenth century, were possessed of magical powers, and legends grew up around the names of Albertus Magnus and Roger Bacon which bear a family resemblance to the Faustian legend of a later day. Moreover the people canonized their own saints, regardless of Rome, including men of action such as Simon de Montfort, and scholar-administrators like Robert Grosseteste, bishop of Lincoln, who had stood up to kings and popes. In the fourteenth century the teaching of an Oxford scholar, John Wycliffe, became widely known and was preserved among the people after it had been suppressed at the university. It led to a demand for the Bible in English and the right to learn directly from it, rather than from doctrine as expounded in church.

It was, however, the growth of urban communities that provided permanent occasion for more developed forms of life, for the interplay of ideas and the spread of knowledge. These were the arena for new educational developments in the twelfth and thirteenth centuries, in the first place for the formation of guilds of scholars, or teachers, which came to be called universities.

The town brought together a number of men sharing the same occupation, who had formerly been scattered singly in small communities, and the common interests of a shared trade or profession led to close association. Guilds formed to defend the interests of a particular calling were interested, in the first place, in controlling methods of entry and this, in turn, implied providing a recognized form of training to qualify the new entrant. By establishing customary rights, and gaining confirmation of these by charter, guilds became the recognized governing bodies of professions and supervisors of vocational education.

This kind of education had a direct effect in forming the social structure of the later middle ages,[40] for towns drew recruits to trades from the countryside, at first the poor but later sons of the gentry seeking a start in profitable merchant undertakings. Schools sponsored by the major churches also drew pupils from quite far afield.

In the town the popular festivals of the agricultural community were recreated. There is a description written in about 1180 of celebrations in London on Shrove Tuesday, the day of the Easter festival particularly dedicated to youth.[41] In the morning cockfighting was the main sport, as it remained a sport for schoolboys for centuries.

> After dinner all the youth of the city goes out into the fields to a much-frequented game of ball. The scholars of each school have their own ball, and almost all the workers of each trade have theirs also in their hands. Elder men and fathers and rich citizens come on horseback to watch the contests of their juniors, and after their fashion are young again with the young.

The writer goes on to note that every Sunday in Lent 'young gentles' would ride out on horseback, while, from the city gates 'burst forth in throngs the lay sons of citizens, armed with lance and shield', in order 'in mimic

43

contest' to 'exercise their skill in arms'. This recalls the warrior initiation of an earlier age.

Summer feastdays also provided an occasion for 'leaping, archery and wrestling, putting the stone, and throwing the thonged javelin'. In winter, 'when the great marsh that washes the northern walls of the city is frozen, dense throngs of youths go forth to disport themselves upon the ice'.

The background of young men, who disported themselves in this way, was a society in which poet and minstrel had for centuries been the purveyors of literature and history. They could, therefore, also take easily to the learning of schools which, in the twelfth century, turned to classical literature including poetry. Indeed this aroused a passionate interest, making the learning of Latin worthwhile. Some felt in almost personal touch with the subjects of classical poets, it has been said. Dido, queen of Carthage, became a popular heroine. Students took her to their hearts, 'wrote lament after lament for her, cried over her as the young men of the eighteenth century cried over Manon Lescaut'. In this sense the classics of the ancient world were always a problem for the church. One of St Augustine's confessions was that he had shed tears for Dido.

It was in pursuit of a knowledge that was relevant as well as attractive that young men sought out schools and began to move from one to another, particularly in France where literary studies were much cultivated. One crystallized the experience when he recalled, in later life:

those first days when youth in me was happy and life was swift in doing and I wandering in the diverse cities of sweet France, for the desire that I had of learning, gave all my might to letters.[42]

44

Similarly, the first mention of Oxford as a resort of students, in the 1180s, has anything but an exclusively academic flavour. It concerns the public reading by Gerald of Wales—a royal clerk of mixed Norman and Welsh parentage—of a tract for the times, a report of his recent journey through Ireland with the king, which was written in lively style in the Latin of current speech.[43] This he read in public, in three parts on three successive days, to assembled students and their masters and townspeople, and each reading was accompanied by public entertainments. 'It was indeed,' he exclaims, savouring the occasion, 'a costly and noble function, for it was, in a way, a renewal of the genuine old times of the poets, and neither during the present age nor in days of old has England witnessed such a spectacle'.

The universities: guilds of teachers

It is one of the chief merits of Rashdall's great history of the European universities that he seeks their social origin, and finds it in the movement towards association which swept through the towns in the eleventh and twelfth centuries. He also provides an account, in this sense, of the framework within which university studies developed.[44]

Once a number of scholars had gathered together practising the common profession of teaching, the development of a code of customs naturally followed. It had long been usual, in settled schools, for the master to hand on his office to his most promising pupil; it followed that one of the earliest unwritten rules was that a new master be initiated to the profession with the sanction of his own teacher. A second principle flowed from this, that the new

45

teacher must have followed a recognized course, not only under an authorized master but for a specific period of time; five to seven years seems early to have been expected.

The preparation completed, the actual ceremony of initiation to the profession was a concrete manifestation of these two principles. The prospective master had the biretta, the badge of mastership, placed on his head and received from his former master an open book, a ring, a kiss and benediction. He was then seated in the master's chair from which he delivered an inaugural lecture. This was the inception to the mastership, the recognition of a newcomer by other members of the profession and his formal entry upon his functions by actual performance of his duties. The inceptor then made the offering of a new entrant to his colleagues—the gift was often gloves —and entertained them to a banquet.

This system had much in common with initiation to knighthood which developed at the same period, and similar forms were adopted by crafts or mysteries. When a ceremony of conferring degrees was introduced by universities it bore traces of the idea that graduation formed a kind of intellectual knighthood. Meanwhile students practised their own initiation rites among themselves, sometimes brutal and often deplored by their elders but too strong to eradicate.

It was not until the second half of the thirteenth century that Oxford university was legally constituted, as a corporation with certain rights and duties in controlling its own affairs. At this point the first college for clerks studying in the university schools was endowed, by an ecclesiastical statesman, and it was expressly for his kindred. The eight original entrants to Walter de Merton's 'house of scholars' at Oxford were all his nephews, and

46

others of his kindred were to make up the numbers to twenty. Only failing such applicants were places open to 'honest and capable young men', and the same applied to a school for fifteen boys attached to the college.[45]

Later founders made similar provision, if on a lesser scale, for young kinsmen who had formerly found maintenance among the dependents of the great household. So old obligations were fulfilled in a new form. There were, however, few colleges for secular clerks before the fourteenth and fifteenth centuries. On the other hand monastic houses established hostels for inmates studying in the schools, and the new orders of friars sponsored by the papacy established their main bases there. Consequently universities, which had gained relative independence from bishops and cathedral chapters, were partially occupied by religious communities belonging to various orders and the faculties of theology were dominated by the work of their scholars. It is only necessary to recall the Dominican, Thomas Aquinas, and the Franciscans, Duns Scotus and William of Ockham.

As the universities settled down to an ordered programme of teaching, different faculties were established each under its group of teachers. The preliminary one, preparing for higher faculties and providing for many who studied only for a year or two, was the faculty of arts, concerned with grammar, logic and 'philosophy'—to which we may return later. The higher faculties covered three fields of immediate importance to the society of the twelfth and thirteenth centuries. These were law, which substituted mind and pen for courage and the sword in settling disputes and underpinning the social structure; medicine, in growing demand as the standard of life rose and larger communities developed; and scholastic theo-

47

logy, not concerned with doctrinal matters in the narrow sense so much as with weaving classical philosophy in with developing Christian doctrine to promulgate a whole ideology.

The establishment of the universities marks a step on to the high road of development. For the medieval university maintained a relatively unchanged form for some six centuries, dominating also the practice of grammar schools—a pattern not yet altogether outgrown.

Education and the social order

In so short a survey, covering so large a subject over centuries, there is a danger of oversimplifying developments. But there is something to be said for a broad approach to break free from the traditional description of the origins and early development of education in England. Its history does not begin in 597, when Augustine landed on the Kentish coast with the Latin prayer book in one hand and the Latin grammar in the other. This merely marks the introduction of a special form of instruction, geared to the needs of an organized Christian church, which met and merged with ways of upbringing which had been in operation for centuries.

This survey has suggested that the initiation of youth is one of the most important social functions. It is from the simple form of education developed in a unitary social order that the elaborate institutions of advanced societies ultimately derive. The tribal form of initiating youth to adult status is closely integrated with the way of life as a whole, or shaped by a common outlook, within a strictly circumscribed world whose fund of knowledge is correspondingly limited. Like all activities in the relatively primitive society, education is sanctified by tradition, or takes its place within a pattern of practices which in sum reflect the society's conception of what life is about. These ideas find expression in a symbolic, or religious, form. But beneath particular and varying ritual the basic pattern is the same—that of introducing the new generation to social practice and the accumulated knowledge of the community, with emphasis on skills relevant to the age group concerned and the place it will take in an adult world bonded by kinship and graded by seniority.

As the communal form of society gives place to a society divided into rulers and ruled, education ceases to be unitary and is differentiated according to position in the social order. In early Anglo-Saxon society, it might be said, in the light of the outline given, education rested on allegiance and the kindred, the two main social bonds or supports of the social order. This was the base for further development, and from here a continuity can be traced both in the upbringing of the nobility and, in vaguer and more general terms, popular upbringing, both grounded in the household. It is interesting to note that the age of seven, commonly accepted in tribal society as marking the end of childhood, remains the generally accepted age for boys to pass out of the care of women and enter on a course of training.

This society's conception of what life is about found expression in and through the Christian religion. In connection with this a particular form of initiation to the priesthood was introduced but this did not remain a closed system, as is usual at a more primitive stage. Rather, in a developing society, it broadened out to spread an influence through the social order, in the measure that the church was integrated with social life at all levels.

49

To approach the matter by this route is to begin to understand what Christianity was to medieval society. It was not merely the outlook of the church, a particular institution, nor by any means confined to religious matters alone. It was the form in which the social outlook found expression.

More than this, the very means to expression were cultivated in this context, through the teaching of grammar, rhetoric and logic. This moulded language itself, and the forms of literature, not merely learned works in Latin but, by a process of interaction, poetry in the native language and everyday speech as well. To take a single example, it is impossible to juxtapose absolutely the sacred and profane, insofar as 'profanity' merely signifies misuse of Christian terms.

Here was a vast machinery of education, of which organized centres of learning might, at an early stage, be seen as a power house. But clearly this is not the beginning and end of the matter.

That formal schooling is established for a particular purpose does not imply that all other forms of education cease. They continue to operate at different levels and the schools, however influential, constitute only one element, the more so since they are still relatively few and far between and restricted to instruction in Latin. Also a social institution, indeed a leading one, is the form of education provided for the nobility in the great household; so, at the other end of the scale, is the training to participate in religious observances which is the only provision society, or the ruling order, now makes for the ordinary man.

However, family upbringing continues at this level and must be counted, for from it will develop an organized form of domestic training in apprenticeship. Also to be reckoned with is a growing divergence between the two poles of society, one of which is associated with literacy and learning, the other dependent on oral transmission; though this does not prevent interrelation, or interaction, between the more sophisticated and the popular traditions.

With the close of the great era of invasions and migrations the hidden strengths of this society become apparent, in economic and social development and also in educational terms. As towns come into prominence popular forms are recreated in specialized guilds, which provide for recruits to particular occupations a directly relevant training. Among these is teaching, originally the primary function of the church but now becoming a professional function.

That the universities remained under the overall control of the church throughout the middle ages, indeed up to the nineteenth century, should not be allowed to obscure the significance of this emergence of professionalism. The later development, on similar lines to universities, of the Inns of Court in London, marked the advent of the first lay profession, that of the common lawyers; their allegiance was to the crown and they played the major part in subjugating church to crown in the sixteenth century, at the Reformation.[46]

This form of education marks a breakaway from household upbringing into the wider world, though the base of apprenticeship to trades remained supervision in the household which extended to manners and morals as well as instruction in special skills. In the earlier middle ages the great lay households were centres of training for secular pursuits of all kinds, as well as the special upbringing of the nobility. The great religious communities provided opportunities for scholarship within their walls and administered schools geared to the needs of the church. In the later middle ages there were two universities, at Oxford and Cambridge, and the guild of common lawyers had its centre near the city of London where were the leading companies of merchants and craftsmen covering training for their occupations. The next step was for wealthy laymen to endow schools, or boroughs to initiate one, while even small fraternities in rural parishes played a part in furthering the instruction of children in the elements as literacy became more sought after. So, gradually, the church's monopoly of education was undermined.

Changing ideas about education

To look ahead is to find that, at the Reformation, the church's position in society is questioned and its powers severely curtailed. At the same time, schooling is reorganized and clearly directed to meeting lay needs. With the establishment of schools serving localities, the best of which have organized programmes of study end-on to the basic university course, the foundations are laid of a system of education in the modern sense. This system comes under the general supervision of the state, to which the church is now subordinate, and is open to adjustment in terms of prescribing what is taught or controlling access to schools insofar as the machinery exists for the purpose. This naturally gives rise to ideas about education in terms of the function it fulfils, or should fulfil, in society.

There was little room for such ideas in the period that has been discussed. Forms of education were modified or established in response to social pressures but, on the whole, taken for granted. The social order was regarded as unchangeable, like the order of nature, and this implied that upbringing should fit the young for the position in society into which they were born, as, in the main, it did. True, some men of humble birth rose to high office in the church, and so the state, on the foundation of a sound education, but their status derived not so much from learning itself as the patronage of kings. The leading ideas were those of the dominant aristocracy, an hereditary nobility by virtue of blood or birth, and it was not imagined that their quality could be improved upon.

In the circumstances education could not easily be seen as something that can change individuals for the better, let alone change society. There was only a slow working towards this idea, from the ground floor, and once more in the towns which fell outside the pattern superimposed on a developing society. Here, in due course, wealthy merchants have a choice of professions and trades for which to train sons, as well as an immediate stimulus to teach them the elements, since literacy is important to the conduct of business and the affairs of the city. And so a planned progression of an educational kind begins to become apparent. Children are brought up at home, sent to school at about seven, and afterwards trained for a chosen occupation.

This careful planning brought results and the example was followed. As educated men, lacking noble birth, came to the forefront in increasing numbers, there was room for a new idea about what education could do. So it was that Erasmus, chief spokesman for educational reform in the early sixteenth century, could pour scorn on the idea that tribal emblems of lineage are the ultimate proof of worth. Only education, which develops qualities of mind and spirit, confers nobility. 'Let others paint on their escutcheons, lions, eagles, bulls, leopards [he wrote in a *Little Book of Good Manners* for children]. Those are the possessors of true nobility who can use on their coats of arms ideas which they have thoroughly learned from the liberal arts.'[47]

With this went a new conception of education as the necessary ground-base from which to realize a truly Christian society, governed by well-educated Christian statesmen and ministered to spiritually by a learned church freed from worldly concerns. What differentiates the modern from the medieval attitude is, then, a recognition that education fulfils an important social function and should be so organized as to engender, or reflect, the values of society. In other words, once an organized system of education becomes established, social and political currents flow through it, now aiding, now obstructing further change.[48]

Ideas, once clearly formulated, can be taken up with effect, sometimes at long intervals. In sixteenth-century England the new concept of education was reinforced by the adoption of a reformed faith which brought the teaching function once more to the forefront, looking back to the practice of the early church. Since protestant doctrine is grounded on the Bible it could be argued that all men have a right of access to the word of God in this form, and so to literacy.

This might be seen as the genesis of the later claim that education is a human right, which in turn recalls the common initiation of all members of the new generation to the social heritage in the unitary society.

Part Two

2

The framework of education

This brief survey has suggested that many and various developments contribute to education, from the rise of towns to the detailed constructions of language. But key questions have only been touched on and some of these can be considered more closely by turning to specialist studies which bridge the gap between different disciplines, and so are of particular assistance in broadening study of the history of education.

History and its branches

Since history aspires to cover the whole spectrum of thinking and action in the past historians rely on many branches of study, though as yet there is not always clarity about how best to bring the findings of different disciplines into relation.[49] The main trend has been an opposite one, for history to throw out branches in all directions which then develop on their own lines. Such are economic, constitutional, ecclesiastical history at one level; or history of law, religion, economic thought at another. As new pressures come to bear, or new fields are opened up, new branches appear: the history of agriculture, urban history, industrial archaeology, demography.

But there is now something of a drawing together and most historians also see the need to come to terms with anthropology and sociology, as has been attempted in some measure here.

Some historians believe that history can have no dealings with science, but the fact is that the historical approach is integral to science. If one wants to discover why something happens, it is necessary to find out how it 'comes about'; i.e., to discover the antecedent conditions which are necessary for it to occur and sufficient to bring it about.[50] This approach is crystallized in the procedure of scientific enquiry in every sphere—natural, human, social. At another level it is crystallized in different branches of history—the history of art, science, medicine, architecture, technology, music, literature—which try to throw light on how and why these different activities have developed to their present stage in order to arrive at a better understanding of their nature.

It is in this context that we find the origin of the history of education at the turn of this century.[51] But this branch of study was only established in departments and colleges of education at the turn of this century.[51] But this branch of history departments of universities; nor is there any way of assessing the place of education in the historical process in the standard history of a period grounded on documentary sources and centred mainly on political events. There is, however, a material difference in the treatment of early history because, given the shortage of surviving documents, historians are forced to turn to other types of evidence and find ways of weaving them together. Students of Anglo-Saxon literature and classicists have also turned to ethnography, or anthropology, with effect. It is on work of this kind that the account so far given has drawn.

In addition it is possible to turn to more specialist historical studies which incorporate different approaches, and there are some which bear closely on education even if this is not the main concern. Such are the three monographs drawn upon in the following pages in order to discuss in more depth themes only touched on so far.

The first theme taken up is the agricultural round, the foundation of society for many millennia and still the context of education for the majority in many areas of the world. The account draws on a study of the thirteenth-century English village by an American medieval historian who is also a sociologist, G. C. Homans.

The second theme is the urban outlook, associated with more specialist forms of work in a different framework, which covers ways of educating children that mark a break with traditional practice. This account is based on a study of the writings of Florentine merchants of the early fifteenth century by a French historian, Christian Bec, who uses techniques developed by social historians in France as well as those relating to analysis of literary forms.

The third theme is teaching in the medieval university, as it persisted more or less unchanged up to the seventeenth century—and in some aspects still persists in university and grammar school. This account rests on a study of medieval scholasticism, in the light of attempts to break it down in the sixteenth century, by an American historian of ideas at this period, Walter J. Ong, a member of the Jesuit Order.

The acknowledgement is made in this form because to draw on sections of substantial monographs—and supplement the account with particular illustrations—does not do justice to originals which are closely argued over a much wider span than is here covered. The following short accounts should be seen, therefore, as inspired by the works drawn upon rather than accurately reflecting their intentions and conclusions at every point. The method is one possible way of absorbing new insights and so bringing the history of education up to date in this sense, and may encourage attention to many other relevant studies which do not necessarily have the word 'education' in the title.

The agricultural year: rural experience and upbringing

Writing about the peasant youth of Russia, living under conditions approximating to those of medieval England, Leo Tolstoy underlined the need to transcend the limited viewpoint of the 'pedagogue'—that education is what teachers decide is best and goes on only in schools, which are directly at war with the depraving conditions of home, street and locality.

'It is time we recognised,' wrote Tolstoy, 'that these conditions are the chief foundation of all education, and, far from being inimical and hindrances to the school, are its prime and chief movers.' And he went on to paint a picture of the peasant child in his own surroundings and at the academic school which concentrated on formal instruction and strict discipline.[52]

It is enough to look at one and the same child at home, in the street, or at school: here you see a vivacious, curious child, with a smile in his eyes and on his lips, seeking instruction in everything as he would seek pleasure, often expressing his thoughts clearly and forthrightly in his own words; there you see a worndown, reticent being, with an expression of fatigue, terror and *ennui*, repeating with his lips only strange words in a strange language.

Tolstoy was inclined to idealize peasant life, but his basic point remains, that a schooling imposed by the educated for a limited purpose, on those whose way of life they despise, is not an education in human terms but runs counter to life. This was in some degree the case with the medieval school, whose chief object was to inculcate Latin grammar on given lines and whose masters came to be distinguished by the birch. There is still a tendency to see a 'grammar school education' as something given and unchangeable, an ultimate measure of what teaching should be. And in October 1969, the headmaster of one at Leicester beat a whole class of twenty-four boys, some of whom had been noisy, as 'a matter of routine'. [53]

Few children from the medieval English village reached any school. If they had any formal instruction it was usually only in following the Latin mass. They were born 'ignoble and degenerate', in the words of a twelfth-century royal clerk, and it was deplorable that a few did manage to rise to high office through the church because the rich were too proud or too lazy to put their sons to school. [54] It was usual, then as now, for men who had themselves climbed successfully to deprecate any extension of the process which might undermine the status so hardly won. Moreover it was easier then, than it is now, for the cultured man, having undergone many years of education and become highly literate in the process, to look down contemptuously on the lower orders. For he spoke Norman-French, or Latin, the only language of scholarship, they only a fumbling vernacular, and how could this restricted code, used in so circumscribed an environment, embody any intellectual content?

Yet it was English that became the language of the nation and the high were forced to share it with the low. Even university and grammar school teachers came round to it at last, though it took decades to wean them from Latin and from retaining the classics at the centre of the curriculum to the detriment of education.

What, then, was the form of education that sustained humanity among the medieval peasantry, over and above mere existence in the teeth of poverty and oppression? This can only be sought in the general tenor of village life as it bore on childhood experience and upbringing. Here it may be recalled how heavy an emphasis Plato laid on the 'unconscious education' of the populace, and his wish to ban poetry and drama from the ideal republic lest they stimulate undesirable ideas. The medieval church was in no position to control popular culture to this extent and could only work to direct it into desirable channels, not always with success.

The village and the children It needs an effort of imagination, on the part of those living in a predominantly urban society in an age of technological revolution, to envisage the medieval village as it was for centuries, in a Roman Catholic country whose economy was grounded on agriculture.

Over large parts of England the main method of farming was the open field system and the pattern of work was constant. A spring crop of barley, oats, peas, was sown in February; a winter crop of wheat and rye was sown in October. Stocks of sheep and cattle were sustained on the same fields, in the intervals of sowing and harvesting, their number controlled by the available fodder and the extent of additional meadowland. The rule of life was maintenance of the agricultural round. There was little stimulus to modify it, or margin to expand the production of crops or livestock in villages which comprised some twenty-five to fifty households. More influential than technology in this society was climate, and the attendant dangers of famine and pestilence. Social life was conditioned by these factors. This way of life has been described, as it was in the thirteenth century, from the point of view of the husbandman.[55]

Most husbandmen held their plots of land in the open fields in bondage; that is, on condition of giving so many days a year to work for the lord of the manor as and when required. But they also worked their own lands and regulated matters of common interest to the village. Village officials were of the community as well as acting in part for the lord. In the manorial court differences were settled by appeal to a jury of villagers, cognizant of all the details of a communal local life, before judgment was passed by the lord's representative. The harsh realities of serfdom were, therefore, mitigated by a measure of self-government and there was some contact with literacy and attendant techniques. This system children could observe in action.

The centre of many communal activities was the parish church in which mass was celebrated daily on behalf of the community. Though expected to attend mass on Sundays people were only required to communicate on three occasions a year—Christmas, Easter and Pentecost—and many did so only before death. The communal religious exercise reflected a way of life in which people were in and of their setting rather than seen, or seeing themselves, as individuals. When, in the thirteenth century, recognized surnames become common men are often identified by their place in the geography of the village—atte Ford, Grove, Well, Townsend—or by their trade; though sometimes characteristics figure, for instance in the name Turnpenny, which then marks a family down the centuries.

It has recently been argued that there was little or no conception of childhood in the middle ages, at any rate by comparison with later centuries.[56] There was unlikely to be the same recognition of a special form of preparing youth for adult life, as at the earlier stage of tribal society, given many upheavals and changed conditions. Indeed, it is often the case that a more coherent form of popular education is found in communities that have suffered the least disruption of traditional ways of life and accordingly have a richer cultural heritage—in parts of Scotland, for instance, by comparison with England at a later date.

In tribal society a rough distinction can be made between aspects of the traditional lore handed down orally to the new generation. This has to do on the one hand with the history and religion of the people concerned, their understanding of the natural world and the laws whereby the community orders its affairs; and, on the other hand, with transmission of the skills necessary to daily activities in household, village and fields. In the English medieval village traditional lore remained only in truncated form, insofar as law and religion were now superimposed from outside; these could only be understood by the illiterate in the measure that they were seen to operate in the community, in parish church, manorial court or village assembly. But there remained the narrower task of induction into domestic and working skills which still devolved on the family.

Judging by the size of houses, the single family unit of parents and children seems to have been common, with kindred connections at the village level.[57] Within households which must provide for all needs—baking, brewing, spinning and so on—children tend to have a specific place by reason of their economic contribution at their own level of ability. This is an important and necessary one outside the household as well, insofar as in agricultural work many hands can be used, indeed are essential at certain seasons; to this extent children are assets over and above the heir who will carry on the family holding of land.

That boys were regarded as 'of age' at fifteen is suggested by the fact that at this age they could succeed to a holding after a father's death. So far as the church was concerned they were admitted as communicants at fourteen. But work in field and household must have begun much earlier and was particularly required in the harvest months. There were also tasks appropriate to the young such as minding poultry, sheep or cattle when the numbers were small and little skill required. In open, hedgeless fields cattle put out to graze after the hay had been harvested could stray into the still growing grain crop, or sheep could move into meadowland reserved for other purposes. To control them was a responsible task, assigned to the village 'hayward'. But the duty is recalled in the nursery rhyme of 'Little Boy Blue'.

Many folk songs incorporate memories of past ways of work or observances, some of which eventually became the prerogative of children. Such were the house to house collections on All Souls Day—'pray good mistress a soul cake'—and Christmas carolling. But no doubt children were of the company when the observances were more general. On the other hand boys and girls in older age groups were brought forward in festivals centred on youth which had a relation to mating and marriage.

This brings to attention the fact that regular festivals were the heart of rural life and that these remained essentially popular observances, despite the addition of a Christian colour. Indeed most of the main feast-days of the church calendar were superimposed on the age-old observances of agricultural communities and to this extent villagers retained a stake in creating the pattern of life and immunity from serfdom of body and spirit. Even today, it may be recalled, the official quarter-days of what has for four centuries been a Protestant country have essentially Catholic titles—Lady Day, for instance, and Michaelmas.

From Michaelmas to Christmas The agricultural year ended and began at Michaelmas, 29 September, ecclesiastically the feast of St Michael and All Angels. The first task in October was ploughing, then sowing of the winter crop, completion of which was marked by the feast of All Hallows, 1 November. Here was one of the four ancient feasts of northern Europe dating from well before the Christian era, which marked the close winter season and was held in honour of the dead. The cattle must be brought in from the fields for winter and to protect them from evil spirits—usually those of the dead—required intercession. The church, failing to modify this pagan practice, settled for 2 November as All Souls Day, but the people continued to celebrate Hallowse'en, and to dance in the churchyards, the gathering place of the dead, despite prohibitions.

66

In general, it was on the eve of feast days, or the whole night before, that popular celebrations were held, so reversing the daily round of the husbandman who retired early in order to rise at dawn. 'Wakes' still survive in various forms, in different settings, whether as funeral observances in parts of Ireland or holiday weeks in Lancashire towns.

From Hallowse'en it was ten days to Martinmas (11 November), associated with the slaughtering of cattle and salting down of meat. This must have brought some reasonably exact appreciation of animal anatomy at the practical level. Indeed, farmers necessarily had their own form of practical astronomy and botany as well as zoology. Then the agricultural task was threshing of last year's harvest, stored in the barns.

The ecclesiastical year opened at this point, for Martinmas also marked the beginning of Advent which continued up to Christmas. This was a twelve-day festival lasting until Epiphany (6 January), celebration of the birth of Christ being superimposed on the pagan ceremony of Yule. One of the main breaks of the year, the Christmas holiday, brought a suspension of servile duties. Feasting was in the hall of the manor on Christmas Day, the fare being provided by 'gifts' in kind brought by the serfs; from the hens, a traditional offering at this season, descend the turkeys of current celebration, just as Easter eggs perpetuate another gift in kind. There were seasonal games a characteristic of which was suspension, or reversal, of everyday rules—epitomized in the election of a lord of misrule, a custom carried over into other communities, such as the universities.

Ceremony and folk song Children had a special place in

this festival, for 28 December was 'Innocents' Day' with which the feast of the patron saint of boys, St Nicholas (6 December), tended to be amalgamated. When Henry VI founded Eton college, with a dependent school for boys, he dedicated it to Our Lady and St Nicholas; hence both 6 December and Lady Day (25 March) were kept as 'founder's days' both at Eton and King's College, Cambridge, and possibly still are.

Here, and in cathedral churches, the ceremony of installing a boy bishop was observed, followed by an organized tour in surrounding villages. The practice was finally ended at the Reformation, by a proclamation of Henry VIII which deplored such 'superstitious and childish observances' in which 'children be strangely decked and apparelled to counterfeit priests, bishops and women . . . and boys do sing mass and preach in the pulpit . . . rather to the derision than the true glory of God or honour of his saints'.[58]

A ceremony which involved conduct of the sacred mass by a choirboy may seem strange. The church usually condemned popular observances which suspended the normal rules of life—such as the dressing of men as women in folk dances. But this one possibly represented an attempt to transfer to a better purpose habits that could not be obliterated, though in the later middle ages the ceremony deteriorated to much the same level as the observances it had been designed to replace.

In the popular mind amalgamation of the sacred and secular seems to have implied friendly familiarity rather than contempt. Derision there might often be—of monks, friars and rich clergy—but popular verse humanized the central figures of the Christian faith as equals. In one folk song, 'The Bitter Withy', Mary's child behaves like any other:

> As it befell on a bright holiday
> Small hail from the sky did fall.
> Our Saviour asked his mother dear
> If he might go and play at ball.
>
> At ball, at ball, my own dear son,
> It's time that you were gone,
> But don't let me hear of any mischief
> At night when you come home.

The gravest of mischief follows: the child vaunts his supernatural status, to counteract jeers at his lowly birth from three pretty lordlings, and uses it to bring about their destruction by drowning. Apprised of this, Mary responds as a village mother.

> So up the hill and down the hill
> Three rich young mothers run,
> Crying: 'Mary mild, fetch home your child,
> For ours he's drowned each one.'
>
> So Mary mild fetched home her child
> And laid him across her knee,
> And with a handful of willow twigs
> She gave him slashes three.

And this is why the willow is the first tree to perish at the heart. There is said to be only one pictorial representation of this story, in a fresco at Lucca.[59] But many folk themes have a European scope, similar ones recurring with local variations at widely different points. After all, the economic realities of the agricultural year were the same and so was the overriding desire of the peasant to ensure regeneration of the soil by which he lived. Everywhere the year was marked by rites of preparation, augmentation and harvest. Everywhere, it may be supposed, children played in the intervals of the tasks assigned to them—given freedom from famine and plague—for this is the characteristic mode of activity of the young child.

Plough Monday to Hocktide The resumption of work after the Christmas holiday was marked by the celebrations of Plough Monday (7 January) descended directly from magical rites which can be traced back to at least the sixth century. In many thirteenth-century villages guilds of husbandmen held a feast on this day, drew a plough round the village collecting pennies and with the proceeds kept a 'plough-light' burning at a shrine in the parish church. Here was a forerunner of parish guilds some of which supported small village schools in the later middle ages. While ploughing was for men, the husbands of the soil, the distaff stood for the 'huswife's' work at the hearth which was also recognized in customary rites. The place assigned to women's tasks is also illustrated by harvest rules which exonerate the housewife and those supervising small children from work at this time when all other hands were mobilized.

Candlemas followed, on 2 February, ecclesiastically the feast of the Purification of the Blessed Virgin Mary, agriculturally the time to prepare for spring ploughing and so for augmentation rites. Shrove Tuesday, marking the beginning of Lent, was a major agricultural holiday, particularly centred on youth and their sports, celebration of which was carried over into the towns, as has been seen. By Lady Day, the feast of the Annunciation, the spring sowing was more or less completed and at Easter came another week's agricultural holiday. Though this was the high point of the church's year, the festival retained the name of a pagan goddess.

Much has been written about the Easter ceremonies of the church, to which the origins of drama have been traced, and, like others, they engaged young and old. At the close of Easter week came Hocktide, a folk festival. This pattern prevailed for all the major holidays—an ecclesiastical ceremony, a week free from labour, rounded off by the popular festival which retained its traditional form.

Mayday to Midsummer's Day The lighter, or less consistent, work of early summer—weeding of crops, sheep-shearing and so on—allowed for more occasional holidays and May was very much a holiday month. It opened with Mayday, essentially the festival of youth and another inheritance from the pagan past, which was adopted as a labour holiday in the nineteenth century.

Rogation days provided a second break, the three days before Ascension Day, or 'holy Thursday'. At this time it was customary to beat the bounds of the village, or parish. The procession of inhabitants with banners and lights was headed by the priest carrying a cross and at every 'holy oak or gospel tree' a prayer for the crops was offered. Small boys were likely to remember the occasion for they were often thrown into brooks or ponds, or bumped against trees and rocks at strategic points, to drive in a knowledge of the parish boundaries. The third May feast was Whitsun, when the first fruits of harvest could be offered, or in Christian terms Pentecost, marking the descent of the holy spirit on the apostles of Christ.

With June came sheep-shearing, completed before Midsummer Day (24 June), ecclesiastically the nativity of St John the Baptist. This was the day when the sun could be seen to reach the highest point of its circle before descent. Small boys patrolled the fields with brands and marked the occasion by setting fire to a cartwheel which was then rolled downhill. On St John's Eve boys were also busy collecting rubbish to make bonfires whose smoke could best ward off the dragons which poisoned springs. The sighting of a dragon in Northumberland is recorded in the Anglo-Saxon chronicle and the saving of a people from the depredations of dragons by the hero is a leading theme of *Beowulf*.

Harvest There now opened the busiest season of the agricultural year in which children were fully involved. It began with haymaking up to Lammas (from the Anglo-Saxon 'loaf mass') on 1 August. Then came the corn harvest, culminating with the ceremony of the 'last sheaf' and harvest home feasting. While there is a vivid description of a sixteenth century sheep-shearing celebration by Shakespeare, in *The Winter's Tale*, the long continuity of harvest home observances is marked by George Eliot's account of the Poysers' farm supper in *Adam Bede*. Up to the nineteenth century the experience of the majority of English children was still grounded in the pattern of the agricultural year, and the same may still be said of millions of children in other countries.

Only the major festivals have been noted. Every parish also had its own 'wake' on the eve of the day belonging to the saint to whom the church was dedicated. This might be a local notability of an earlier age, canonized by popular acceptance rather than papal edict. The Leicestershire village of Wigston, for instance, had a church dedicated to St Wistan, a Mercian prince who met with his death at nearby Wistow in 849; this later served as village schoolhouse while services were held at the more regularly dedicated church of All Saints. Another popular saint was Swithun, a bishop of Winchester in the ninth century and reputed teacher of King Alfred. His day (15 July) is still taken as a guide to whether or not the harvest will be threatened by rain.

Other dates related to preparation for marriage. Such were St Agnes' Eve (20 January, recalled by Keats), or St Valentine's Day (14 February), supposedly the day birds begin to mate and so one for exchange of love tokens, but which accidentally acquired the name of a Christian martyred in third-century Rome.

All these regularly recurring festivals aided the maintenance of a vernacular culture, enriched and modified down the years, and so firmly rooted. Work itself stimulated efforts to master the round of the seasons and understand the nature of animal life, crops and the materials used by village craftsmen. But there was no means of generalizing such experience and popular wisdom remained at the level of traditional lore, passed down in pithy sayings, or was incorporated in skills which were handed on as such to the younger generation.

Religious instruction In this general context, religious instruction was less a stimulus to thought or skill than an addition to ritual invocation, for the teaching of children was primarily related to the Latin mass or the memorizing of prayers.[60] The elements of number may have entered into consciousness by way of the chief matter of popular instruction which fell into numbered groups of sins and their antidotes. The church enumerated the seven deadly sins—covetousness (the sin of the world), gluttony, sloth and lechery (sins of the flesh), pride, envy and wrath (sins of the devil). To these three main types of sin there were three sovereign antidotes—fasting (to subdue the flesh), almsgiving (to counteract covetousness), charity (to vanquish the devil and his works). Under the last two of these heads came the seven works of mercy, to which recognized forms of charity approximated: feeding the hungry, providing drink for the thirsty, clothing the naked, harbouring the wayfarer, caring for the sick, relieving prisoners, burying the dead.

A good deal of this was more relevant to the education of the rich than the poor. But for the latter especially there were the saints, friendly guides often with a local habitation, or willing to supervise almost any particular group. Thus St Giles cared for cripples, St Leonard for prisoners, St Nicholas for boys, St Katherine for girls.[61]

In the circumstances images of the saints and mural paintings in church may have conveyed more through the eye than the Latin service conveyed through the ear. The church was in and of the community in a way difficult to appreciate now. Not only was it a regular meeting place, even on occasion storehouse, but its bells carried messages to the fields and accordingly became personified with their own proper names.[62] But this personification of inanimate objects was a more general tendency, indicating again lack of a clear distinction between human beings and their surroundings in the order of nature.

The peasant outlook Work in agriculture, the foundation of medieval society, reinforced certain ways of thought. Characteristic of this mode of life is a tendency to see the future in terms of the past, to conceive of movement in cycles equivalent to the agricultural year, and of human life following a similar cycle from birth through the different 'ages of man' to death. Corresponding to this are ways of preparing the young to fit into social life, as it is and will continue to be, and this form of upbringing has few specific features. In a restricted peasant community it is also subject to few intellectual influences. An oral culture lays most stress on memory but the visual also counts for much, as it is beginning to count for more today. This is not to say that logico-empirical thought is absent, even though it may only be directed to specific aspects of work. Indeed, it is to be found even in primitive tribal society, and today, given a relevant education, children born into a tribal community step into the modern world with relative ease. A relevant education may be defined as one that equips children with the techniques of learning, by contrast with traditional didacticism tailored to impart only what those in charge think it desirable 'the folk' should know.[63]

Medieval England was a backward country with a low level of literacy, in which the great majority were caught up in a vicious circle of underdevelopment from which their betters had no inclination to release them. On the contrary, most teaching and preaching was directed to persuading them that unremitting toil was the lot God had appointed for those at the base of society, tempered only by the promise of something better in the world to come, if dues were properly paid to the church. Yet the people made something of life in this world, in their own ways, and the record requires attention insofar as it throws light on the basic conditions of education for the majority of children.

A good deal of sentiment has been engendered about

the folk and their ways, by well-meaning folklorists as well as academics influenced by a certain school of literary criticism who never tire of regretting the passing of the village wheelwright's shop; though, no doubt, they would rapidly have tired of working in one. Nor is there much call to sentimentalize about the civilizing influence of a medieval church which too often fell short of its own standards, particularly in the later middle ages. What is more deserving of attention, so far as popular education is concerned, is the way oppression was kept at bay by retaining a hold on the pattern of life and so also the vernacular oral tradition. This conferred a comparative immunity to teaching and preaching beamed from outside—as may even be the case today, despite all the modern technology of education—and ensured the maintenance of a distinctive popular culture and outlook.

Ways of work and life fostered a certain understanding of the nature of things, even if prevailing ideas and the language in which they were expressed did not assist in furthering understanding. But the village was not completely isolated; it had its operative links with the wider world through manor house, monastery, in particular the neighbouring market town. Town and country life were essentially interdependent, exercising a mutual influence, and this opened the way to development.

For the countryman the urban community provides a different model, against which he can measure his own experience, or which enables him to see it more objectively. He may not necessarily admire and wish to emulate, he may be moved to gain literacy in turn. But the point is that the very existence of the town creates a conception of 'country' life, as a particular mode rather than life itself, the only way.[64]

In this context the peasant outlook emerges in sharper relief. In particular, at a time when technical aids are few, the worker in agriculture tends to see himself as part of nature, as working with the elements rather than 'confronting' them; accordingly his tendency is to placate, since he lacks the means to coerce, to value security above adventure, to surrender to providence rather than tempting it—and these attitudes are handed down to the new generation. It is from this 'philosophy' that the townsman tends to break away.

Yet a basic acceptance of the natural order, sanctified by the church as divinely ordained, remains at the root of much intellectual activity in medieval society, even in the highest realms of scholarship. That man and his society are part of a given order of nature, that the human mind directly apprehends this natural order (which, in reality, it creates in the process of assimilation), these were key ideas in scholarship and teaching; just as co-operation with nature, rather than intervention to change its course, was the operative way of life of the majority working on the land. In short, society binds all together, the limitations imposed by the way of life affect all its members. Despite the convolutions of intellect, the educated can be as fast prisoners as those whose work supports them in their specialized activity.

The urban outlook: civility and the education of children

The basic reason for the establishment of the medieval town was trade, or merchandise. The merchant conducts a business which depends, to a greater or lesser extent, on keeping records and accounts. Here is a strong stimulus to literacy absent in the rural setting, where written records are the province of the manorial court and occasional needs can be met by a single member of the community, whether parish clerk, priest or schoolmaster. But over and above this specific stimulus, life in the relatively developed urban community provides new opportunities for, and engenders new attitudes to, learning and education.

This has already been suggested in general terms in discussing the rise of the university. The church might preach original sin and degeneration, but men gathered together in the new conditions of the twelfth century pursued knowledge in the light of an opposite idea—the power of reason to raise humanity to new heights. So a contemporary schoolmaster could write:[65]

> The animals express their brute creation
> By head hung low and downward looking eyes;
> But man holds high his head in contemplation
> To show his natural kinship with the skies.
> He sees the stars obey God's legislation,
> And learns the laws by which mankind can rise.

In the later middle ages wealthy citizens in the greater towns of Europe had a relatively high standard of living and, particularly in the merchant centres of the Italian peninsula, there was a developed civic organization and consciousness. Some members of a literate and active merchant class in Florence committed to writing thoughts about educating children and these may be taken to represent the urban outlook. It was one formed over and against the traditional outlook to which the moral teaching of the church approximated. As may be recalled, it was customary to represent medieval society as composed of those who fought, those who prayed, and those who worked. There was no clearly defined place for those who bought and sold, accumulated capital, adventured over-seas, governed towns and built up family life in this set-ting to establish new standards for aristocrats.

Florence was a city with wealthy merchants whose business carried them far afield; indeed, a city state with a strong civic sense born of specific conditions. But all towns developed a civic outlook in some measure and it is the purpose here to trace basic attitudes, the product of urban living and engagement in trade, which transcend particular circumstances. In London similar attitudes may be discerned in embryonic form at the same time—the late fourteenth and early fifteenth centuries.[66] But in the sixteenth century much was learned of the educa-tional practice of Italian city-states through the writings of scholars, and this helped to hasten developments in England. To this extent the analysis of trends is relevant at two levels. It is also more generally relevant in that there are many ideas about education today which derive from the general outlook of different social strata, though the underlying attitudes and assumptions often remain unexamined. To make the connection in one context may help to do so in another.

Towns were recruited from the countryside. Even the well-established town constantly received new entrants who set up in trade and adapted to life as members of the urban community. The town kept its own records, branch-ing out from the legal and administrative to the chronicle of events and the doings of leading citizens. The first or second generation tradesman, whose family was putting down new roots, sometimes contributed to this process by drawing up a family record. It came naturally to record not only the background and progress of the family and

79

its business, but the lessons learned from experience in the form of technical and moral advice. And this advice was framed with the coming generation, and experience of bringing it to maturity, in mind. It is on records of this kind that the following outline is based.[67]

Upbringing in the merchant family Whereas the countryman's concern was preservation of the land, which provided the means to life in return for labour, the merchant's primary need was to ensure the continuance of the family business, the context of his work for a livelihood. This implied, in the first place, continuance of the family itself in such a way as to provide worthy successors. Accordingly the merchant is advised to take great care in choosing a wife, and, since sensuality is bad for the woman and resulting children, to be moderate in his sexual life. Domestic life must be well regulated both as a background to efficient business and as the base for bringing up healthy children with a sound moral outlook.

The new generation will take over the running of a business which calls for the exercise of various qualities of mind and character, in particular the ability to mix easily with others up to and including the wise and powerful who run the city's affairs. It should be the aim of parents to find ways of developing these qualities. Therefore education should be generally directed to perfecting the art of communication and, more specifically, to fostering the individual skills and attitudes needed in business affairs.

These propositions, argued in practical terms, underline the merchant tendency to measure both actions and sentiments by the returns they bring, i.e., by the test of practice. This pragmatism is evident in the more general advice from which educational ideas derive. Since the merchant needs the trust and approbation of his customers, particularly his wealthiest customers but also those of all kinds, his aim must be to make no enemies and acquire many friends. He should, then, be of good appearance, courteous, equable and not eccentric. On the other hand, he should also avoid timidity and conformism. Good business demands the breaking of new ground and this calls for judgment and strength of character. These are among the qualities that education should develop.

Pragmatism and rationalism Merchant pragmatism derives directly from ways of work. Merchants must chart new routes, quite literally sometimes in terms of taking commerce to an unknown area, but also in more general terms. By comparison with the young country-man who depends on a long community experience and a given pattern in agriculture, repeated over the years, the young merchant operates on his own account, depending primarily on the particular experience of his father. Basing himself on this he learns, in turn, from his own individual experience in action.

The kind of work he does is likely to require the exercise of initiative in particular situations, the balancing of possibilities before making a firm decision. When a merchant meets with ill-fortune, rather than submitting to it and losing all his assets he must come to grips with the situation and look for a way out. This calls for energy, versatility, a readiness to take control of events.

It will be seen that this adds up to rejecting, in practice, the traditional idea of a providence which shapes all ends and lives. While this idea may accord well enough with the husbandman's experience, whether of the ravages of natural elements or the legalities governing his tenure of land, merchant experience leads to the forming of a different outlook, components of which can be traced in the changing use of terms in merchant writings. The active entrepreneur, rather than submitting to a larger will for want of any alternative, exercises his own will-power, using his reason in the light of experience. In other words, faced with a particular difficulty, the merchant must be able to review past experience, make a balanced accounting of the factors in the situation and in the light of this work out what to do. It follows that education should develop the power of reasoning in relation to con-crete situations.

The change of attitude may be traced in more general terms. Merchant activities are concerned with concrete returns, in business and social life. The more immediate returns there are in this world, the less need for the promise of reward in the world to come. Even eternity can be attained at the secular level, insofar as the man who is successful in family and city life has his name entered in the records for posterity. This also brings a modifica-tion of religious outlook. Whereas the general mass serves the village community, the merchant enters into a private contract with his God, by making donations for special masses, particular gifts to charity and so on, representing advance payment for services solicited or a return for services rendered.

Literacy and civility All this adds up to a practical and moral outlook which is inculcated by education in the merchant household. Literacy is a practical necessity so young children are taught to read and write, as a prelim-inary to technical training in apprenticeship to the family business. More generally necessary is an apprenticeship in the art of communication beginning with active participation in the community of the household. This is a first step in acquiring social behaviour of the kind needed to succeed on the stage of public affairs.

A young man who has mastered the art of communication with others has prepared the way to gain experience from older and wiser citizens and so can readily do this when he enters the wider world of social life. By participating fully in that life, with a readiness to exchange experiences and learn, he himself acquires practical wisdom. This is a central feature of the educational ideal of 'civility', born in a civic setting. It may be contrasted with 'courtesy', the behaviour acquired in aristocratic circles, though the two terms tend to come together in the measure that the two classes concerned meet and mix.

In considering how to bring up his children to succeed in a particular milieu, the head of the merchant family learns to look at his child as a child. By comparison with rural life, changing little through one agricultural year after another from youth to old age, merchant life is highly variegated and different moments in it are valued separately. There is also a recognizable preparation for it. As a result there can be a new recognition of childhood, as a stage in human development, and a close interest in problems specific to this stage the answers to which shape the pattern of early upbringing.

Parental responsibility Central is a recognition of parental responsibility for good upbringing, of the mother for small children and girls, of the father for forming his sons. A new departure, by contrast with current educational methods, is recognition of the need for love and understanding rather than force and fear, and pragmatism enters into this. Beating children detracts from their freedom to develop without effectively disciplining them. This is an unproductive method, from the point of view of both the immediate and long-term results desired, and as such to be avoided.

Parents should try to ensure that a child develops his own particular characteristics, for individual character is an asset in social life and such active qualities as will-power are needed in business. Boys also need confidence and adroitness and these can be fostered by practising different forms of sport. Equally, by practising social behaviour in company a boy can overcome any tendency to timidity or vulgarity which hamper communication or exchanges in society. It is, above all, by cultivating the key art of communication that he becomes well informed, not merely in a social but a business and political sense. His best course, having learned from his father, is to absorb the experience of other successful citizens, taking them as models and shaping his actions accordingly.

It is in this connection that the study of classical authors, necessitating learning Latin, comes in as a necessary part of education. To read a good author is to conduct a colloquy at will with the wisest men of past history and to draw freely on their knowledge. This crowns the education acquired in active conversation with knowledgeable contemporaries which draws on current experience. Nor need education in this form ever end, for the habit of reading and learning from authors can profitably continue throughout life.

The classical authors recommended are those likely to contribute to the ends desired. Cicero, for instance, wrote about active, civic life, applying rational thought

84

to social and moral matters. Study of such works helps to develop the power of reasoning to a clear conclusion, so necessary to the active man of affairs, and fosters an ability to foresee the results contingent on a particular course of action. It may be noted that to advocate the development of abilities of this kind was to ask for something very different from the kind of logical reasoning cultivated in the contemporary universities. It was to substitute for scholarly wisdom, accumulated and pored over in the study, practical wisdom in the conduct of life.

Criticism of current educational practice These aims or ideals, were rarely so clearly envisaged as this account may suggest, let alone realized in all merchant families in early fifteenth-century Florence. Rather merchant writers advise particular practices which, traced to their source in city and business life, add up to what may be called a bourgeois ethic. As applied to the upbringing of children this dictated methods sharply at variance with those in use in schools dominated by the church.

To take a particular instance, corporal punishment was a prominent feature in schools of the later middle ages, for heavy chastisement was held to mitigate the effect of original sin, or drive the devil out of children. As for what was taught, at the higher levels this had to do with the professional concerns of law, medicine, teaching, all under the influence of the church, and entry to the church itself. Schools tended to fall into line as the initial preparation for such studies or occupations. Methods of instruction, therefore, took little account of individual characteristics or the forming of personality. While the art of logic was intensively taught it was in relation to situations and subjects far removed from practical life.

Games, moreover, were generally frowned upon as epitomizing popular forms of amusement with which the church was ever at war, and so as particularly unsuitable to clerks undergoing instruction in school. It was, then, in direct opposition to much of current practice that the educational outlook described was formulated.

Merchants wrote in a very concrete and empirical way. But the attitudes that find expression in their writings, the propositions they advance, were added to, generalized and elevated into a set of educational principles later in the fifteenth century, by scholars who were themselves of the towns and courts and ardent students of classical literature. Their books were in turn drawn upon, and modified, by northern scholars of the early sixteenth century seeking educational reform along similar lines, or the transformation of schools to provide a relevant education for laymen.

The urban school It was natural that changes in the form of upbringing in the family should result in a new recognition of the power of education and the desirability of extending popular instruction on new lines. This could be done by establishing public schools administered by the city government. At this level, again, the influence of the urban way of life can be traced.

The agricultural year was governed by sun and seasons, one following another in the direction of eternity, measured out in more detail only by festivals or canonical hours. With town and trader the clock came to be part of general life, marking the opening and closing of workshops or counting-houses, making time measurable, amenable to planning, foreseeable. As business was conducted beneath its moving hands there ripened the concept of 'losing time', or 'wasting' it, and when schools were established the aim was to make them more businesslike than before, producing better returns.

Medieval teaching was long-winded and repetitive, moving in cycles without much differentiation of stages. The new lay school was organized in classes, one following another in an ordered progression. This was the pattern introduced to early sixteenth-century London by John Colet and he specifically required that the boys of his school should not 'waste time', either praying in the middle of lessons—as schoolboys had done for centuries —or indulging in 'foolish disputation', the characteristic method of the medieval university.[68] There are similar efforts today to make education more effective, sometimes in the purely philistine sense of getting greater 'productivity', sometimes in terms of making the curriculum more relevant and seeking educational techniques which facilitate learning. It was to the latter point that sixteenth-century reformers in England bent their efforts.

A century earlier Florentine merchants had turned to financing schools for the city's children and to rehabilitating a declining university. For their own sons they employed, as tutors, scholars whose writings generalized, and elevated, their own aspirations. Such men also became tutors at princely courts and translated principles into practice in this setting. It was from this position that there developed a full-blooded attack on traditional pedagogical literature, born of cloister, library and disputation in university schools, which had buried classical writings epitomizing civic ideals, and obscured much practical wisdom under a burden of didactic commentary. For the soliloquy of the scholar, in communication with books, advocates of the new education substituted universal colloquy among men, about matters related to reality and human life.

All this was passed on to England, to merge with experience on the ground, in the early sixteenth century. There resulted schools organized into classes, using new textbooks and methods, which rapidly increased in number. An essential ingredient of their curriculum was the 'colloquy' about matters relating to life, at a level adapted to the experience of children. Attendance at the Elizabethan school was required on every 'working day' and during working hours—that is, between 6 a.m. and 6 p.m. in summer, 7 a.m. and 5 p.m. from Michaelmas to Lady Day—and their business was clearly laid down. Holidays were as clearly demarcated. But these—the twelve days of Christmas, Easter week and Whitsun week—remained the chief traditional holidays of the agricultural year.

Learning and teaching: the legacy of the medieval university

It has been suggested earlier that a turning point in the history of education is the 'professionalizing' of teaching and scholarship, from the twelfth century, in organized schools, or universities. This led to the establishment of a form of education which was much criticized in the sixteenth century and somewhat modified as a result, at any rate in schools. But it proved a much more difficult task to modify university practice which still retains some medieval characteristics today. It is worth taking a closer look at this and how it was consolidated.

In the first place it should be recognized that the medieval universities were not centres of higher education as the term is now understood, or of research at

88

the expense of teaching as is sometimes held against universities today. Their primary concern, which shaped not only curriculum and methods but scholarship itself, was the teaching of intending teachers. To examine the tradition established from this point of view casts light on various problems which are still actual.[69]

Broadly speaking, it was the task of medieval scholars to dig into the store of knowledge inherited from the ancient world, unearth or harvest different aspects and process for use. In the teachers' guilds, which became universities, the recognized use for knowledge was to impart it to the coming generation of teachers. Accordingly the tendency was to process knowledge into a form that made it possible, or easy, to teach. All the key works of the medieval world are, essentially, textbooks with the virtues and faults of the genre in varying proportion— up to and including the *Summa Theologica* of Thomas Aquinas.

As time went on many who studied at universities went on to do other things than becoming university teachers for life, or, even, teachers from the pulpit; and university work was influenced by pressures from the outside world. But it continued to be the case that every student who sought the licence of 'master' must teach in the university schools for at least two years. Thus the B.A. marked acceptance as an apprentice teacher in the faculty of arts, on the road to qualifying as full master (M.A.), and the same applied in the other faculties. In time the B.A. came to mark a degree of learning in a more general sense. But, by and large, courses continued to be shaped to impart, not so much knowledge itself, but knowledge of how to teach.

Grammar may serve as an example. Instead of assisting

students to learn grammar, the university discoursed about the nature of Latin grammar as a subject. The practice filtered down into the schools and generations of young boys, taught Latin by the direct method, conned and memorized an analysis of grammar rather than grasping how to use it. As illustration, this is the form of the *Ars Minor* of Donatus, an epitome inherited from the fourth century in use by children up to the sixteenth.[70]

How many parts of speech are there? Eight.
What? Noun, pronoun, verb, adverb, participle, conjunction, preposition, interjection ...
What is a pronoun? A part of speech that is often used in place of the noun to convey the same meaning and now and then refers to a person previously mentioned.
How many attributes belong to the pronoun? Six.
What? Quality, gender, number, form, person, case.
In what is the quality of pronouns? It is twofold: for pronouns can be definite or indefinite.

And so on.

This also illustrates a basic form of teaching, the dialogue between teacher and learner—or, if you like, the catechizing of the pupil by the teacher, though here it is reduced to a formal dimension for rote learning. This was a general tendency as universities became settled and courses of study established.

The importance of logic In early days the best teachers, those whose reputation resulted in the gathering of influential schools, were polymaths. In the forefront of thought, they also covered the whole range of scholarship, as then constituted, in their teaching. At this moment, in the twelfth century, the logic of Aristotle—

the main aspect of his work then known—was the great stimulus to both teaching and intellectual enquiry. The appeal of logic has been likened to that of 'scientific method today'.[71] To grasp this key was to open all doors, impose order on a disordered world, even plumb the working of the mind itself. Method in thought, logic, provided a closely reasoned and unassailable way to truth. The universities made logic their own and foresaw a time when, by its aid, all knowledge would be ranged in an orderly way and understood.

But, if the method became firmly established, the material to which it must be applied proved more intractable than had been supposed, and, in particular, much more extensive. Not only were there many fresh discoveries of the heritage of ancient learning but what came to light often contradicted established conclusions. Prominent among new discoveries were the scientific works of Aristotle, which upset earlier calculations and resulted in renewed efforts to absorb all the parts of learning into an ordered whole. Moreover this great body of pagan learning must be assimilated to the Christian faith. Since God had created the universe there was reason to believe it was knowable and that to understand it was to reach a deeper understanding of the divine will and purpose. In embarking on this task in the thirteenth century, an age of social advance which provided a direct stimulus to extend knowledge, the universities reached their high point.

It was also at this time that universities became permanently established, with charters, buildings, a relatively permanent course of study set out in statutes. When they settled into a groove, as organized institutions, the great teacher of an earlier age, covering all aspects of the curriculum, had given place to bodies of teachers specializing in particular faculties. Each of these tended to be jealous of its own ground, much as different educational institutions are today.

At the crown of the major universities was the faculty of theology. Other higher faculties relating to the profession of law and medicine were much less important and influential in the northern universities of Paris and Oxford. But the edifice of higher learning rested on what was by far the largest, and in some universities the most powerful, faculty—even if its function was to prepare for higher ones—the faculty of arts.

The primary concern of teachers in this faculty was logic, as it were for its own sake, for the faculty of arts tended to be cut off from higher learning and scholarship which were the province of rival faculties of teachers. Similarly the arts faculty was the province of teachers of 'arts' and their horizons were limited to this level above which they did not themselves pass. What went on in the faculty of arts, however, largely determined the scope of education in schools up to the sixteenth century and beyond.

There is no need to enlarge on what still remains a familiar pattern. But it is worth going into some more detailed aspects of medieval arts teaching, which involve quite complicated points, because this helps to understand other continuing problems.

The course in the faculty of arts It is usually said—and contemporary works concur—that the arts faculty was concerned with the 'seven liberal arts'. These had long been enumerated as grammar, rhetoric and logic (the trivium) and (the quadrivium), arithmetic, geometry, music, astronomy—that is, so far as the latter subjects were understood, though there was virtually only one textbook covering all, Boethius. Moreover the seven liberal arts were often represented pictorially, as if there were an ordered progression from one to another. But the dictum bore little relation to the reality, at any rate after the twelfth century. What arts faculties actually taught was the nature of grammar and rhetoric (as described) together with 'philosophy'.

The term 'philosophy' was taken over from the ancient world but the study it denoted at this level did not correspond at all to the kind of enquiry cultivated by an Aristotle or a Plato. It covered a course which began with logic and passed by way of 'moral philosophy' to 'physics'.

Logic we may return to again later. As for 'moral philosophy', because the arts faculty was warned off ground belonging to the faculty of theology, this tended to be a truncated subject. (This helps to explain how it was that the schools of so Christian a society had no basic text relating to Christian morality; down the centuries the first readers were Aesop's fables and the moral precepts of 'Cato' which incorporated a lore devoid of Christian connotation.)

As for 'physics', this covered an assortment of information and speculation relating to aspects of the natural world, psychology, physiology, taxonomy, alchemy. In effect, therefore, logic did not lead on to philosophical discussion but to a survey of pre-scientific knowledge of various kinds. This completed the arts course. While 'physics' on this model may have been useful to intending doctors of medicine—or physicians—it was of no account for intending lawyers, nor well regarded by theologian-philosophers. If they were interested in scientific and mathematical knowledge, it was on quite another plane, from which the arts faculty compendium seemed mere dabbling confusion. (One might roughly compare the heights of scientific research today with O-level general science.)

In practice, then, the solid core of the arts course became logic—with vestigial remains of grammar and rhetoric at one end, and moral and 'scientific' dictums at the other. This concentration on logic had a formative effect in moulding the pattern of thought.

In considering the intellectual climate, it should be realized that a false picture results from concentrating on the thought of major scholars—and then stringing their ideas together in the form of a connected account of the development of knowledge—leaving aside the authors most studied by contemporaries. (Compare the particular view of English literature which results from stringing together a 'great tradition' of selected works valued by present-day critics.) It has been suggested, for instance, that Thomas Aquinas was probably a good deal less important to medieval scholars than has been thought, or, if his work was valued, it may well have been because it was easy to teach rather than for the quality of thought which now excites admiration. Again, the works of other great doctors of scholastic theology, William of Ockham and Duns Scotus, are hard to come by in surviving medieval libraries, by comparison with now unknown names whose works were everywhere.[72]

It is little to the purpose, then, to study a history of medieval scholasticism—which now has a much higher reputation among modern scholars than formerly—in the hope of getting a picture of the knowledge that formed operational ideas, at the time. Thus the ideas of the medieval arts faculty were formed not by a philosophy bearing on metaphysics and science but by a 'philosophy' bounded by logic. It is easier today than it was to grasp this point insofar as English philosophers—including those who operate in education—have returned to the groundbase of logical analysis, forced from the heights of speculation and validating knowledge by scientific methods of discovery and validation.

Logic is essentially a contributory study, without an idea of its own it might be said, concerned with methods of thought. If no attention is paid to the matter of thought there results preoccupation with making fine distinctions in purely verbal terms, or arriving by formal argument at a verbally irrefutable definition. By its very nature the procedure becomes contentious and has a strong tendency to breed intellectual arrogance on the basis of small certainties. These tendencies were fostered by the disputations which formed the main exercises in the university, in the arts faculty as in others.

Pedagogy—the operational form of knowledge There was no clear distinction between what was taught ('philosophy') and how it was taught (pedagogy). In the medieval university all studies tended to be operational in this sense, as has been noted. Moreover the lack of differentiation between subject and object, implying in turn lack of a concept of the individual, has already been referred to in discussing the peasant outlook. In educational terms it implies no understanding of the psychology of the learner.

Insofar as psychology was discussed it was well below the level of sophistication attained by Aristotle. For practical purposes it was assumed that the categories of know-

95

ledge, as differentiated by logic, corresponded to the configuration of the human mind. It followed that the teacher's task was to present material in a logically organized form for absorption by student minds. The only concession to youth was to offer a boiled-down version, correspondingly tasteless.

The practice can still be observed in some English grammar schools. Consequently the 'theory' is also still with us, in, for instance, the Crowther Report which asserts that children, particularly clever ones, are 'subject-minded'.[73]

It is difficult to discuss this amalgamation of learner and what is learned (subject and subject of study) because language itself reflects it. Thus 'learning' has a passive sense, relating to what has been accumulated in the past, in books, or minds. But it also has an active sense: 'learning' on the part of the individual, and we have come to distinguish a particular form of learning process in the child. In some languages, as has been noted, the same word stands for both 'learning' and 'teaching'. All this summarizes an historical process.

The surest sign of a learned and wise man is his ability to teach what he knows, said Aristotle. Medieval universities inherited from the ancient world, and the fathers of the church, the idea that knowledge is for teaching. Indeed the church itself rested on the idea that, after God first taught man, it remained for a chosen body—heirs of the original apostles—to continue this teaching to see the world through to its end; an event which, incidentally, was often forecast and sometimes daily expected up to the close of the seventeenth century.

The universities interpreted this task in a professional way. In so doing they replaced the lively dialogue of a

Socrates, the active catechizing of the early church, with the dead wood of logic, or 'dialectic'—the terms are interchangeable. In higher faculties logic might be cultivated in the search for truth, traditionally the overriding purpose of universities, particularly at times when there was a strong stimulus to intellectual activity. But in the faculty of arts, and particularly as the search for new knowledge waned, logic ceased to be perfected as an instrument for intellectual discovery and became simply a subject of the curriculum. Indeed, it shaped a curriculum devised for the purpose of preparing teachers, who then reproduced the process in turn in the university and grammar schools.

As teaching settled into a routine it took on certain forms. Clearly it was impossible to conduct a lively Socratic dialogue with up to fifty students. Hence the monologue, or lecture. This was supplemented by a private exercise, the disputation, which retained the outer shell of dialogue but in practice was a mock battle between two logicians each endeavouring to floor the other in verbal terms. This was the standard exercise, and also the form examinations took for students who were qualifying to get up on the rostrum (or pulpit) and keep an end up verbally there.

Students were often forbidden to take notes at lectures, just as lecturers were not supposed to write these down; this was a 'mystery', not to be shared, and the virtue lay in practice of the craft. Lecturers discoursed on texts by respected authors, much as clerics give sermons on a text from the Bible, and in time the discourse, or commentary, came to substitute for the original text itself. The commentary on an author was the standard textbook of the medieval student. This might be seen as a kind of dialogue, between commentator and original, though all too often the latter was obscured behind the former. But the student reader, or hearer of lectures, became the passive observer at second-hand of a dialogue between others. Hence the call of sixteenth-century reformers for a return to personal contact with great writers and thinkers, to what they had actually said in their own words, and a return also to active, participatory, learning in the form of colloquy and catechism.

From the active to the passive It would seem that the gradual change in the nature of university work in the later middle ages is reflected in the use and meaning accorded to key terms—such as 'doctrine', 'discipline', 'method', 'arts', 'science'. Medieval scholars usually interpreted 'science' as knowledge organized in relation to general principles or axioms; 'method', as the order found within a well organized science; 'art' as the acquired skill of the practical intellect in doing or making over something. *Doctrina* was originally 'teaching'. *Disciplina* was 'learning'.

In the pedagogical situation of teaching a relatively unchanging body of knowledge, these terms took on a predominantly passive sense. Thus 'doctrine' became the matter taught, the unassailable truth, an organized body of knowledge to be accepted as the last word, science itself (theology, it may be recalled, was seen as the highest of sciences). 'Discipline' came to denote the subject taught —as it still does when we speak of different disciplines— or a way of keeping the pupil quiet. As for 'method' this became equated with a scholastic exercise, the disputation, which was the active embodiment of logic—but a logic paraded for its own sake rather than to the end of making a reasoned progression to a clear conclusion.

It becomes obvious why reforming efforts, from the sixteenth century, concentrated at this point in the effort to clear the way for reasoning to a relevant end. One of the milestones on the road from scholasticism to science is Descartes' 'discourse on method'. John Locke flayed the academics and their literally endless disputatiousness.

> Right reasoning is founded on something else than the predicaments and predicables, and does not consist in talking in mode and figure itself . . . Is there any thing more inconsistent with civil conversation, and the end of all debate, than not to take an answer, though ever so full and satisfactory; but still to go on with the dispute, as long as equivocal sounds can furnish a 'medium terminus', a term to wrangle with on the one side or a distinction on the other ... For this, in short, is the way and perfection of logical disputes, that the opponent never takes any answer, nor the respondent ever yields to any argument.[74]

It was in the same spirit that, almost a century before, Francis Bacon had pointed to Aristotelian logic as the chief barrier to the quest for truth. Rather than remaining bonded by the aim of achieving logical consistency in verbal terms, and thus complacent in the belief that great minds have already discovered unaided all there is to know, it must be recognized that thought derives from observation and practice, that its validity can be judged by the test of practice, that it can become thereby a guide to action and the advancement of knowledge. From Bacon's point of view the contemplative wisdom of leisured Greek philosophers, their appropriation of the real world into systems of thought, or bodies of knowledge, then supposed to be absolute and finished, was a form of intellectual arrogance a developing society could no longer afford. Didactic methods of education merely perpetuated the fundamental error.[75]

Here it may be noted that the term 'bodies' of knowledge derives from a moment when the study of anatomy came into prominence; their tendency to become inert in academic institutions adds pertinence to this derivation from the corpse. An illustration of how the didactic aim shouldered out the scientific, even in practical anatomy when ecclesiastical objections to this were overcome, is the procedure adopted. The doctor stood at the lectern calling out the parts of the human body and his assistant simultaneously produced them out of the opened cadaver and held them up to the assembled gaze—so proving how correct the teacher's exposition was. Something of the kind still goes on, under the name of teaching science, in some classrooms today.

At the time, however, the practical demonstration, the presence of something seeable and tangible, was a great advance. Attempts were made in the seventeenth century, by followers of Bacon, to introduce teaching on similar lines in schools, but they resulted in little more than the occasional illustrated textbook. Since words had for so long been used to obscure rather than elucidate, early scientists concentrated on what they could 'see with their own eyes' as the only objective way of attaining 'real knowledge'. At the same time they bent efforts to reducing language to a straightforward report of things as they are, and things as they change under the conditions of controlled experiment. But natural science developed outside the universities so that the educational methods associated with it were also excluded, and, indeed, are only now making a way into the schools.

As educational reformers pointed out in the seven-

teenth century, scientific procedure bridges the gap between theory and practice, bringing together the practical
and intellectual with the creative and aesthetic. The
methods of education evolving in schools today endeavour
to do the same, to ensure that the young acquire techniques
of learning, and experiences which enrich them as human
beings, rather than merely taxing their memories with a
verbal exposition of facts or opinions. This educational
development marks a decisive break with the scholastic
tradition first consolidated all of eight centuries ago. On
the other hand it is interesting to note that universities,
which originated as guilds of teachers, responsible for
apprenticeship to teaching, have in the modern age failed
to prepare lecturers for this function. Nor do they accord
education its due place as a subject of academic importance; even today Oxford has no professor of education and
Cambridge no institute providing higher studies for those
working in this key field.[76]

Epilogue

It has been the aim of this discussion to consider education as a universal process in society, rather than merely in academic terms. Looked at in its historical origins, education is the means of introducing the new generation as a whole to the social heritage, to the sum of the community's experience or its fund of knowledge. Looked at from the point of view of social practice, education has become increasingly differentiated for different sections of the population in the measure that their ways of life have diverged, or the division of labour has operated.

The establishment of institutions of formal education has often tended to underline differences. A basic division in developing societies was that between manual and mental work and it was in the service of the latter that formal schooling developed, with an inherent bias towards verbalism. That few had access to learning in medieval society, while the great majority remained illiterate, favoured the development of a scholarly mystique in an academic world organized on protectionist lines. In this context learning could easily be seen as the special sphere of scholars, rather than a social heritage, something to be preserved rather than advanced, guarded rather than disseminated.

Insofar as social polarization has persisted, and with it the educational deprivation of the majority, so also have traditional learned values. That learning is for the few, vocational preparation for the many, has remained a leading idea in modern industrialized society, conditioning the development of the educational system. Consequently the great expansion of re-organization of formal education over the years has not brought a corresponding change in time-honoured attitudes and didactic methods, so much as providing an extended field for their deployment. It has proved a tremendous task to overcome the deeply ingrained verbalism of tradition, which has made school something of a purgatory for generations of children. Only with the pressures of an accelerating scientific and technological revolution is the medieval grammar school finally being superseded and traditional methods displaced. With this goes a readiness to recognize that education begins in home and locality and that schooling should relate to life.

Less generally recognized is the need for scholarship to relate to life, rather than according solely with the habits of scholars. Such was the staying power of scholasticism in the ancient universities, self-governing corporations able to keep reform at bay, that only with difficulty did science gain an entry in the nineteenth century. Even then it was only accepted as junior partner in the academic establishment and the scholastic approach has persisted in traditional departments of scholarship, to exercise an influence also on newer studies. As a biologist has observed: [77]

Historians, literary scholars, even social scientists, approach many problems as they do, not because this is an effective way but simply because that is the way that has been followed since medieval times. They have a terrible impulse to begin an investigation as did the scholastics by saying 'Now let us define our terms.' The more fruitful scientific attitude is to say, 'Here is something peculiar; let us study it. Definitions can wait until we know more about the phenomenon.'

This is a relevant method of approach to education which has yet to be comprehensively studied to the extent that some far less important fields have been investigated, though definitions of it have not been wanting. A fruitful way of discovering more about this phenomenon is by historical study of its changing forms, and related changes in the concept of education, for this is to draw on the actual experience of promoting and thinking about the education of the young. To do so is to provide a framework for relevant judgments, or for appraising education in a meaningful and objective, as opposed to a formal and subjective, way. For those working in education, in particular, there is no better way of standing aside from present practice, in order to see it more clearly in the round, or of resisting that tendency to sanctify past practice which has so often hamstrung educational institutions down the years.

It is always difficult for those directly involved to judge of educational values objectively, as the historical record illustrates. In the early sixteenth century fellows of Oxford colleges, capable only of teaching scholastic logic, were beside themselves when new classical studies were introduced and forecast the downfall of both religion and learning—

some beating the pulpit with their fists for madness, and roaring with open and foaming mouth, that if there were but one Terence or Virgil in the world, and that same in their sleeves, and a fire before them, they would burn them therein, though it should cost them their lives.[78]

In the nineteenth century teachers of classics felt much the same about science. Nor are parallels lacking today.

Logical disputations went merrily on at the universities in the late seventeenth century, at a time when lively minds were turning to new forms of study. No doubt those who fostered them intended to impart something worthwhile but, cognizant only of a relatively cloistered world, their judgment was unequal to the task. Habit played its part. Quite intelligent dons enjoyed the highpoints of disputation on ceremonial occasions, much as devotees of all-in wrestling savour particular muscular tensions and throws which to the average man seem senseless brutality. But the modes of thought inculcated, or engraved into youthful brains, positively inhibited the movement of thought in relation to movement in the world at large. And this might be seen as the negation of education.

Here is sufficient warning against assessments of education, or educational values, from a purely academic point of view. By looking at the process of education in terms of the young generation as a whole, and the actual nature and development of educational institutions, it is possible to arrive at an understanding of the *operative* educational values in society. This enables a realistic judgment not only of past and present practice but of present and future educational needs.

Notes

1 The researches of Russian neurophysiologists and psychologists have directed attention to this point and emphasize the key importance of speech in mental development; see A. N. Leontiev, 'Principles of Child Mental Development', in *Educational Psychology in the Soviet Union*, ed. B. and J. Simon (1963).

2 C. M. Cipolla, *Literacy and Development in the West* (1969).

3 The following paragraphs draw on George Thomson, *Aeschylus and Athens. A study in the social origins of drama* (1941), ch. vii, Initiation. The social nature of these rites should be noted, as against Freudian insistence on the biological aspect of puberty, even though it is not at puberty that initiation takes place. cf. A. van Gennep, *The Rites of Passage*, trs. M. B. Vizedom and G. L. Caffee (1960); Raymond Firth, *We, the Tikopie. A sociological study of kinship in primitive Polynesia* (1936), pp. 423 ff.

4 Gordon Childe, *What Happened in History* (1942), p. 214.

5 Jack Goody and Ian Watt, 'The consequences of literacy', in *Literacy and Traditional Societies*, ed. Goody (1968), pp. 42-55.

6 Marion Gibbs, *Feudal Order* (1949), pp. 29-30.

7 Tacitus, *Germania*, trs. H. Mattingley in *Tacitus on Britain and Germany* (1948), pp. 111-12. For evaluation of this evidence and a discussion of later developments, H.

M. Chadwick, *The Origin of the English Nation* (1924).

8 This section draws on a vivid description of social forms at this stage in H. M. Chadwick, *The Heroic Age* (1912). See also Dorothy Whitelock, *The Beginnings of English Society* (1952).

9 A. L. Poole, *Obligations of Society in the XII and XIII Centuries* (1946), pp. 32-3.

10 In the still standard work by P. Guilhiermoz, *Essai sur l'origine de la noblesse en France* (1902). cf. Carl Stephenson, 'The origin and significance of feudalism', *American Historical Review* xlvi (1940/1) p. 806; Marc Bloch, *Feudal Society* (trs. 1961), p. 313.

11 For an analysis of the evidence in surviving texts, Lorraine Lancaster, 'Kinship in Anglo-Saxon society', *British Journal of Sociology*, ix (1958), pp. 230-50, 359-77. That historians should pay more attention to the matter is argued by D. A. Bullough, 'Early medieval social groupings: the terminology of kinship', *Past and Present*, No. 45 (1969).

12 Quoted in Whitelock, p. 94.

13 *Anglo-Saxon Poetry*, ed. R. K. Gordon (1926), pp. 54-5.

14 Homer, *The Iliad*, trs. E. Rieu (1950), pp. 172-4.

15 See R. W. Chambers (ed.), *A Fifteenth Century Courtesy Book*, Early English Text Society, Old Series, Vol. 148 (1914).

16 The system is described in Sir John Fortescue, *De Laudibus Legum Anglie*, trs. and ed. S. B. Chrimes (1942), p. 119; for abuses of it, from an early date, A. L. Poole, pp. 96-103.

17 For a description, R. W. Southern, *The Making of the Middle Ages* (1953), pp. 107-10.

18 M. Deanesley, *Augustine of Canterbury* (1964), pp. 42, 55.

19 F. Stenton, *Anglo-Saxon England* (1946, 2nd ed.), p. 135.

20 For marriage, G. Le Bras, 'Canon Law', in *Legacy of the Middle Ages*, ed. C. G. Crump and E. F. Jacob (1926), pp. 344-9.

21 J. H. R. Moorman, *Church Life in England in the Thirteenth Century* (1945), p. 81.

22 Chadwick, *Heroic Age*, pp. 425-6.

23 For Pope Gregory's instructions to this effect, Bede, *Ecclesiastical History of the English Nation* (Everyman, 1910), pp. 52-3.

24 A. L. Lloyd, *Folk Song in England* (1967), p. 96.

25 *Life in Shakespeare's England*, ed. J. Dover Wilson (1944 ed.), pp. 45-6.

26 Deanesley, pp. 63-4.

27 David Knowles (ed.). *Decreta Lanfranci: The monastic constitutions of Lanfranc* (1951), p. 110.

28 Bede, p. 283.

29 *Medieval Latin Lyrics*, trs. Helen Waddell (Penguin, 1952), p. 127.

30 *England before the Norman Conquest*, ed. H. W. Chambers (1926), p. 204.

31 See 'The Anglo-Saxon Schools 650-800', in R. R. Bolgar, *The Classical Heritage and its Beneficiaries* (1954).

32 Quoted in E. Legouis and L. Cazamian, *A History of English Literature* (1933 ed.), pp. 13-14.

33 See F. Stenton, chapter vi, 'Learning and Literature in Early England'.

34 David Knowles, *The Monastic Order in England* (1949), pp. 561 ff.

35 D. M. Stenton, *English Society in the Early Middle Ages* (1951), chapter v, 'Church and people'.

36 Southern, p. 188.

37 Gibbs, p. 65.

38 Knowles, *Monastic Order*, pp. 45 ff.

39 G. N. Garmonsway (ed.), *Aelfric's Colloquy* (1939), pp. 13-14.

40 George Unwin, 'Medieval Gilds and Education', in

his *Studies in Economic History*, ed. R. H. Tawney (1927), pp. 92-8.

41   The account, by Fitz Stephen, is translated in F. M. Stenton, *Norman London* (Historical Association, 1934).

42   Helen Waddell, *The Wandering Scholars* (1957 ed.), pp. 24, 134.

43   Quoted in H. Rashdall, *The Universities of Europe in the Middle Ages*, ed. F. M. Powicke and A. B. Emden (1936), vol. iii, p. 25.

44   Rashdall, vol. i, pp. 15, 285-7.

45   Rashdall, vol. iii, pp. 192-3.

46   Joan Simon, *Education and Society in Tudor England* (1966), pp. 53-5.

47   Quoted in Foster Watson, *The English Grammar Schools to 1660* (1908), pp. 105-6.

48   J. Simon, ch. xii, Education and social change.

49   For references to discussions of this question, John Fines, *The History Teacher and Other Disciplines* (Historical Association, 1970).

50   R. Harré, *An Introduction to the Logic of the Sciences* (1960), p. 26.

51   Brian Simon, 'The History of Education', in *The Study of Education*, ed. J. W. Tibble (1966), pp. 103-4.

52   *Tolstoi on Education*, trs. L. Wiener (Chicago, 1967). The translation has been adapted. A new one is in preparation, by Alan Pinch.

53   *Leicester Mercury*, 25 October 1969.

54   A. L. Poole, *From Domesday Book to Magna Carta* (1951), p. 239.

55   Material is drawn chiefly from the chapter, 'The Husbandman's Year' in G. C. Homans, *English Villagers of the Thirteenth Century* (Cambridge, Mass., 1942).

56   Philippe Ariès, *Centuries of Childhood* (trs. 1962); the original French title was 'The child and family life under the ancien régime'.

57   'An excursus on peasant houses and interiors 1400-

1800' in W. G. Hoskins, *The Midland Peasant. The economic and social history of a Leicestershire village* (1957; reprint 1965).

58 Frederic Harrison, *Medieval Man and his Notions* (1947), pp. 162-3.

59 Lloyd, pp. 123-5.

60 For thirteenth century primers of prayers, *Horae Beatae Mariae Virginis* or Sarum and York Primers, ed. E. Hoskins (1901).

61 Glanmor Williams, *The Welsh Church from Conquest to Reformation* (1962), ch. 13, Popular religious beliefs and observances.

62 J. Huizinga, *The Waning of the Middle Ages* (Pelican, 1955), p. 229.

63 For the resuscitation of an almost medieval conception of 'the folk' and advocacy of a correspondingly adjusted form of education for the majority, G. H. Bantock, *Culture, Industrialisation and Education* (1968). Compare M. R. Wedd, *Born for Joy. Teacher and learner in a village school* (1969).

64 R. Redfield, *The Primitive World and its Transformations* (1955), pp. 48 ff.

65 Quoted by R. W. Southern, 'Medieval humanism', *The Listener*, 8 September 1965.

66 Sylvia Thrupp, *The Merchant Class of Medieval London 1300-1500* ch. 4, The conduct of life, and *passim*.

67 It rests on Christian Bec, *Les Marchands Ecrivains: affaires et humanisme à Florence 1375-1434* (Paris, 1967). Part ii, 'Merchant humanism' has a chapter 'Merchant pedagogy'; part iii opens with a chapter, 'Merchants and humanists'. See also Lauro Martinez, *The Social World of Florentine Humanists 1390-1460* (Princeton, 1963).

68 J. Simon, pp. 74, 95.

69 This account draws on Walter J. Ong, *Ramus, Method and the Decay of Dialogue* (Cambridge, Mass., 1958), one chapter of which is 'The pedagogical jugger-

naut'. It should be noted that this study rests largely on material relating to the university of Paris; cf. Gordon Leff, *Paris and Oxford Universities in the Thirteenth and Fourteenth Centuries* (1968).

70   *The Ars Minor of Donatus*, ed. W. J. Chase (Madison, Wis. 1926).

71   Southern, *Making of the Middle Ages*, pp. 171-3.

72   *The English Library before 1700*, ed. F. Wormald and C. E. Wright (1958), p. 91.

73   *15 to 18*, vol. i (1959), p. 223. The chapter concerned, on the grammar school sixth form, is out of tune with the rest of a report which is far from traditionalist as a whole.

74   Quoted by Southern, pp. 175-6, from John Locke, *Thoughts concerning Education* (1690). For the text of actual disputations in the late sixteenth and early seventeenth centuries, W. J. Costello, *The Scholastic Curriculum in Early Seventeenth Century Cambridge* (Cambridge, Mass., 1958), pp. 19 ff.

75   B. Farrington, *Francis Bacon: philosopher of industrial science* (1951), pp. 93-7, 146-9 also his *Science and Politics in the Ancient World* (1939).

76   Brian Simon, *Education: the new perspective* (1967), p. 19.

77   Edgar Anderson, *Plants, Man and Life* (1967 ed.), p. 123.

78   Quoted in J. Simon, p. 84.

Bibliography

This selected list (to add to works mentioned in the notes) relates to the main issues covered in the text, under headings differentiating separate and not always coincident branches of study. A useful bibliography covering all aspects of English life in town and country—homes, dress, work, pastimes, folklore, education etc.—is *Local History Handlist*, ed. F. W. Kuhlicke and F. G. Emmison (Historical Association 1965; revised 1969).

Pre-history, Ancient History, Archaeology A general introduction to pre-history, Gordon Childe, *Man Makes Himself* (1956). A. R. Hands, *Charities and Social Aid in Greece and Rome* (1968), ch. v. D. Talbot Rice, *The Dark Ages* (1965) synthesizes archaeology, history of art, history. Drawing heavily on archaeology, with many illustrations, R. H. Hodgkin, *A History of the Anglo-Saxons* (2 vols, 1933); M. and C. H. B. Quennell, *Everyday Life in Anglo-Saxon Times* (1959).

Anthropology Margaret Read, *Children of their Fathers. Growing up among the Ngoni of Nyasaland* (1959) has a useful select bibliography. M. Fortes, *Social and Psychological aspects of education in Taleland*, International African Institute Memorandum No. 17, 1938 (reprint 1969) is by a one-time psychometrist now Professor of Social

Anthropology at Cambridge. For current problems of scholarship, Lucy Mair, *An Introduction to Social Anthropology* (1965). For use of anthropological techniques in modern Britain, beginning with rural communities in Ireland and Wales which retain many traditional features, Ronald Frankenburg, *Communities in Britain. Social life in town and country* (1966), with full bibliography.

Psychology For a psychological approach within the framework of social history, L. Vigotsky, *Thought and Language* (Cambridge, Mass., 1962); also A. R. Luria, *Speech and the Development of Mental Processes in the Child*, ed. J. Simon (1959; reprint 1968), ch. i. A comparative study of children from different cultures, P. Vernon, *Intelligence and Cultural Environment* (1969).

Methodology and Philosophy For alternative approaches to history, E. H. Carr, *What is History?* (Penguin, 1964) and G. R. Elton, *The Practice of History* (Fontana, 1969). An illuminating critique of the social sciences, Hugh Stretton, *The Political Sciences* (1969). In *Education as Initiation* (1964), R. S. Peters takes over this key term, without reference to its anthropological content, and turns it to the uses of analytical philosophy.

Folklore Folklorists have published much interesting information about English customs but no discipline has been established in English universities, though there are institutes in several in America. In this tradition, shading over into anthropology with the most recent volume, is the well-known work of I. and P. Opie on nursery rhymes and games. For folk tales in a raw state, *Grimm's Household Tales*, trs. M. Hunt (Bohn's Standard Library, 2 vols, 1884). For northern mythology, H. R. E. Davidson, *Gods and Myths of Northern Europe* (1964; reprint 1968). For scholarly editions of fairy tales the bibliography to Harvey

Darnton, *Children's Books in England* (2nd ed. 1958). To add to A. L. Lloyd's study, Frank Howes, *Folk Music of Britain and Beyond* (1969), G. Jenkins ed., *Studies in Folk Life* (1969), B. J. and H. W. Whiting, *Proverbs, Sentences and Proverbial Phrases from English Writings mainly before 1500* (1969).

History of Literature When popular forms become fixed, 'English Literature' takes over; for instance, D. C. Fowler, *A Literary History of the Popular Ballad* (Duke University Press, 1968); Hardin Craig, *English Religious Drama in the Middle Ages* (1955). Earlier scholars had an extensive knowledge of the literatures of Europe and allied studies, notably H. M. Chadwick and W. P. Ker whose *English Literature: Medieval* (1912) remains an excellent introduction.

History of Art, Architecture, Music In the new series 'Planning and Cities', Douglas Fraser, *Village Planning in the Primitive World* (1970). Relevant to visual and aural education, R. L. P. Milburn, *Saints and their Images in English Churches* (2nd ed. 1957); R. W. Tristram, *English Medieval Wallpainting* (2 vols, 1944/50); L. Harrison, *Music in Medieval Britain* (1958) and other such works.

Economic and Social History: Local History Notable recent studies are D. A. Harvey, *A Medieval Oxfordshire Village: Cuxham, 1240-1400* (1965), R. H. Hilton, *A Medieval Society: the West Midlands at the end of the thirteenth century* (1966). See also the books of the pioneer of local history, W. G. Hoskins. There are histories of towns of all kinds—market, corporate, monastic, cathedral. To come nearer to the family environment, M. W. Barley, *The English Farmhouse and Cottage* (1961).

Demography: the family Practically nothing has been done by English historians to investigate the basic unit on which civilization has so largely depended: see Joan Thirsk, 'The Family', *Past and Present*, No. 27 (1964). Central to family life and child upbringing is the status of women, Eileen Power, 'The position of women', in *Legacy of the Middle Ages*, ed. C. G. Crump and E. F. Jacob (1926), and *Medieval People* (1924). D. M. Stenton, *The English Woman in History* (1957), and, given features which prevailed over centuries, Alice Clark, *Working Life of Women in the Seventeenth Century* (1919).

History of Law and Government   P. Vinogradoff, 'Customary law', in *Legacy of the Middle Ages* (1926) and papers on Canon and Civil Law in the same volume. Brian Tierney, *Medieval Poor Law: a sketch of canonical theory and its application in England* (1959). There has been virtually no attention to local government since S. and B. Webb, *History of Local Government: Parish and county* (1924); see also H. F. Westlake, *The Parish Gilds of Medieval England* (1919).

Medieval History: England and Europe   Still a good way in are two short books in the Home University Library, H. W. C. Davis, *Medieval Europe* (1912; revised 1960), Sir Maurice (F.M.) Powicke, *Medieval England 1066-1485* (1931; reprint 1969). And the best symposium, *Legacy of the Middle Ages*, ed. C. G. Crump and E. F. Jacob (1926; reprint 1969). There are detailed bibliographies in volumes of the *Oxford History of England*, short ones in the *Pelican History of England*; see also the *Cambridge Medieval History*.

Ecclesiastical History   Since this is central during the early medieval period it is covered in general histories. There are several books by M. Deanesley on the early church. The historian of English monasticism is David Knowles who has written many books. His *Christian Monasticism*

116

(1969) starts from the beginnings in the desert and goes up to the problems of English monasteries running large public schools today; chapters of his *The Evolution of Medieval Thought* (1962) amount to a history of education. For the church as teacher, G. Howie, *The Educational Writings of St Augustine* (1969). For reforms introduced by the Roman Catholic church in the sixteenth century, and their bearing on education, John Bossy, 'The Counter-Reformation and the people of Catholic Europe', *Past and Present* No. 47, 1970.

Biographical Studies　These often range widely. A recent one of a key figure, Peter Brown, *Augustine of Hippo* (1967). Some older works have not been superseded: *Bede, his life, time and writings*, ed. A. Hamilton Thompson (1935), G. F. Browne, *Alcuin of York* (1907), F. S. Stevenson, *Robert Grosseteste, bishop of Lincoln* (1899). More popular are several books by E. Duckett on Anglo-Saxon saints and scholars.

Intellectual History: History of Education　The history of ideas—or intellectual history—has been very much the province of American scholars until recently. There is a useful selected booklist in H. Wieruszowski (ed.), *The Medieval University* (1966). Other selections of documents, also from America, are: L. Thorndike (ed.), *University Records and Life in the Middle Ages* (New York, 1944), D. Herlihy (ed.), *Medieval Culture and Society* (1968) with useful introductory material. Developments in England from the twelfth century are covered in John Lawson, *Medieval Education and the Reformation* (1966). An illustrated sourcebook, Robert Alt, *Bilderatlas zur Schul—und Erziehungsgeschichte* (Berlin, 1960), vol. i, begins from tribal initiation; *Pictorial History of Education and Schools* (1961) gives an English translation of the texts to the illustrations.